Hidden Messages

Decoding Past Hurt to Unlock New Beginnings

I0148929

Shanteria Tipler

You Never Know How Strong You Really Are Until Being

Strong Is Your Only Option. ~Bob Marley

Life Chronicles Publishing
Give your life a voice!

www.mylifechronicles.org
Life Chronicles Publishing
ISBN-13: 978-0998911441
ISBN-10: 0998911445
Cover Design: Life Chronicles
Editor: John A. Huguley
Life Chronicles Publishing Copyright © 2017

Contents

Introduction

Every day we're faced with decisions to be made. Whether that be taking or leaving a job, confronting that coworker, where to live, all the way down to what we decide to wear. What if I told you those decisions derived from hidden messages we received throughout the course of our lives? Hidden messages that consciously and subconsciously play a part in how and why we operate in the manner we do. These messages can be negative or positive. For the purpose of this book, we are going to tackle those messages which place you in compromising situations and cause you to have a hard time setting boundaries. Messages that create a war inside of you and try to convince you that you're not worthy of love. Messages that silence you and stop you from exercising your right to speak out and to protect yourself. In this book, you will go with me through dark valleys where I felt powerless, helpless, worthless, empty and downright debauched. You'll see how some of the messages I received as a child were being confirmed in different situations I found myself in. You'll see how I was being drawn to those things that fed what I had already subconsciously believed. Join me as I decode my past in preparation for my new beginnings.

Acknowledgments

To my Heavenly Father: I can do all things through you who gives me strength. This book is a testament to that. For every sleepless night and painful situation, I say thank you. Thank you for seeing me fit to carry the message. To believe enough in me that I could go through the valley and stand on the mountain telling the good news. I dedicate this book to your people, all those whom this is meant to touch. May your love, grace, forgiveness, and comfort be felt by each heart that encounters this book.

To every person who has ever endured the waves of life: I wrote this story for you. When I began this journey, I had not yet realized the seeds that would be planted. I watched as my tears watered them and they began to take root eventually being birthed into a lotus flower.

To my beloved Husband: Who would imagine we would go through such a storm and come out more in love then we were before. Thank you for seeing me the way God saw me. For embracing who you knew I would be even before I saw myself in that light, and for standing with me despite my imperfection. I couldn't ask for a better husband. You inspire me to be all that I was created to be. I love you.

To my sister Nyabella: You have seen me at my lowest and have stood in the gap for me when I could not stand on my own. There are no words possible to describe my gratitude towards you. Life would not be the same without you. I love you with everything in me. You are my rock.

To my family, friends, and church loved ones: It is almost impossible to navigate through the twist and turns of life without a support system. You all have surrounded me and kept me lifted through some of my darkest hours. Thank you for your continued prayers, words of encouragement, correction and for all the times you pushed me to keep going knowing that where I was headed was better than where I had been. It truly takes a village. Blessings.

To my lotus flowers, though you have been rooted in mud and detached from the source in which is necessary for nourishment you are getting ready to rise above the surface to bloom into a remarkable beauty.

Chapter One

A Mothers Love

Every girl dreams of playing in mommy's makeup, walking in her high heels and being tucked in after her favorite bedtime story, but as for me, well that wasn't in my deck of cards. You see, mom was a single mother of four children all of whom had unique personalities. She kept us in the latest fashions and made sure we were always presentable. She was very big on image in our house. Let's just say our house looked like something straight out of a magazine. We got lots of compliments and "you all are so lucky" remarks from peers. Though on the outside I was well put together I felt shabby on the inside. I'm talking thrift store, homeless man, dusty kind of shabby. I didn't understand how I could be laced in the most expensive threads yet feel so worthless.

As a little girl, I spent a lot of time overcompensating for what I was reminded that I lacked. I was what you would consider the ugly duckling. I was 50 shades of black with teeth arrangements something like a horse, and to add insult to injury I had this deep raspy frog-like voice. I remember the first-time mother brought to my attention that my features stood out and not in the way one would want them to. It had been raining the entire morning, and I watched as the sun started to peak from behind the last cloud right through the window onto mama's nicely decorated living room.

"You're always doing something you're not supposed to," she commanded, "Now go sit your black ass down somewhere."

The heaviness in her tone jolted me back to reality. For the life of me, I couldn't understand why she chose to add those two words, "black ass" as if it gave her request any more life than it already had. As time went on my skin color would typically be the go-to when a derogatory statement was being made or the "66 teeth" in my mouth as she would say.

A tall, slim caramel mocha woman. My mother's skin was flawless, her smile was indescribable, she walked with the confidence, and she never stepped foot out the house without being immaculate from top to bottom. She had a certain je ne sais quoi about her. Every guy wanted her, and every woman wanted to be her. Along with her finesse, she was extremely bright. Although she was a great student, her focus was one thing and one thing only, money. When she wasn't working or going to school, she would be at the casino or on a date with John, no wait Bill, or was it, Mike? My mother was no stranger to doing what she had to do to receive the results she desired. I learned at a young age that your body was powerful and held the key to getting whatever it is your heart sought after, and I watched as mother did just that.

"You look, nice mama, where are you going?"

"Out with a friend," mama said.

"Which friend?" I inquired.

"Why you don't know him," mama replied with a mischievous smirk.

One thing was for sure; she had a whole lot of friends. Tonight, is fend for yourself night and make sure that kitchen gets cleaned, she shouted as she put on the finishing touches of her make up.

3

"Find something in there to eat," she added.

That usually meant to create something using condiments and whatever else you could conjure up from the cupboard.

"Yes, ma'am," I responded.

Thinking to myself, this is going to be another late night for her.

The night hour eventually turned into the wee morning, and I was nestled comfortably in bed. Without warning my blanket was snatched off, the first strike landing right across my inner thigh. Mama was home, and she was not happy.

"Didn't I tell you to clean the kitchen before I left?" she asked.

"I did mama."

"You didn't mop the floors," she rebutted.

Which was usually code for it wasn't done to her liking. I took cover as she administered a few more strikes. When it was over I got up and swiftly made my way to the kitchen. The cold from the tile floor felt refreshing against my bare feet, to some degree, it took the focus off my

4

burning welts. That was mothers MO. She didn't care that it was 3:00 am, and I had school in the morning. If it wasn't done to her standards, it was going to cost you and it was usually more than you had bargained for. Kitchen was mopped to perfection, and I scurried back to bed.

The sun came up, and the rays of sunshine greeted my face which meant it was time for school. I was dragging and begging myself to get a move on it.

"Get your ass out of bed! If you weren't so trifling, I wouldn't have had to wake you up to clean up," mama's voice sounded from the door way.

That was enough motivation for me to get up and get out the door. At that point, anyplace was better than there. I made my way to school which was one of my least favorite places, and it showed in my behavior and grades. I was the class clown and for the most part, it helped past time.

"Ms. Simmons, you're disrupting my class again," Mrs. Valdez called out to me. "One more interruption and I will be forced to call your mother."

"Sorry Mrs. V but this class is super whack," I joked under my breath.

"That's enough, out of my classroom!" she demanded.

I knew in the back of my mind that would warrant a call home, but at that moment, I felt like a boss. I thought about the phone call for the rest of the day and I contemplated not going home because I knew what awaited. I took the long route and walked rather slow. I could feel my palms starting to sweat the closer I got to the door. I tiptoed to my room hoping I wouldn't be noticed but it wasn't long before I heard the roar of my Punisher.

"So, you think you're grown huh?" A stern voice questioned from behind me.

"No, ma'am," I replied.

"So why the hell you at that school giving them people a hard time?"

I said nothing. Most questions during the pre-whopping interrogations were usually rhetorical.

"Take your clothes off and face the wall!" she demanded.

I hastily began disrobing and preceded with placing my hands on the wall as instructed.

The beating seemed to go on forever. Mother had a habit of swatting between each word and sometimes her sentences ran long.

"Didn't... I... tell... you..."

After she was satisfied with the amount of punishment inflicted, she headed towards the door. Before exiting, she looked back at me with a cold cadence.

"...and I still love you," she declared.

Those words only seemed to be used in our home after beatings took place. It was to be understood that because I was given nice material things, I should automatically know I was loved and it didn't need to be said. Hence why that proclamation rang like music to my ears in whatever form or fashion, it was delivered. I love you was given so scarcely that I hung onto them for dear life. I learned early that love hurts.

After her departure, I sat on the floor dreaming of the day I would get away from this prison. No one would tell me what to do and I would be in control. The thoughts slowly faded as I drifted off into sleep on the floor but was soon awaken by the breeze of the frigid night air. Slowly sitting up I could hear something coming from the hallway.

I crawled over to the door and put my ear to the small opening. Moanings were creeping from underneath mama's door followed by a high pitch outburst of pleasure. I sat there for a moment as tingles traveled to all my no-no spots. As I came back to reality, there was a howl of release in the form of a male's voice. I don't know who was in there mounting my mother, but I knew his pockets were deep. In that room, no one gets their world rocked without coming out a few dollars lighter. After a while silence filled the house and I returned to bed.

I watched day in and day out as sex and manipulation were used to get into the pockets of men. I saw how they were putty in the hands of their master, all for a piece of what delicately lye between her legs. They were flies stuck in her web and before they even noticed they were wrapped up and devoured. I watched her conquer, and I wanted ever bit of that power. Little did I know she had sold a piece of her soul with ever encounter.

As time went on, my behavior became worst around the house. It wasn't too long after things started to take a turn for the better at school, it felt as though things were starting to look up. I had become known as the dark girl with the big booty. Smack, my butt jiggled as this fine chocolate brother standing 5'9" with waves so deep they could sink the Titanic, swatted both cheeks with the palm of his basketball crafted hand. Hey tabletop, he greeted me, with the grin of a kid in a candy store. Shocked that he was even talking to me, I smiled shyly and looked down at my fingernails, completely negating the fact that he had just touched my booty. Deep down I liked the attention. I saw the excitement in his eyes after he got a touch. It was the same look mama's friends had before going into the hot box. I realized that I had something he wanted, and my confidence slowly began to rise. School was now my favorite place. Somebody was finally paying attention to me, and I felt valuable.

I skipped home after school thinking about the encounter I had with one of the finest brothers at Seaside Middle School. To add a cherry on top I know I had seen him around my apartment complex quite a few times. I was smiling from ear to ear and my heart skipped a beat with every step. Walking through the front door, I was still dazed.

"Samantha, get down here now," came a demand.

The honeymoon quickly ended as my presence was promptly being requested by Cruella De Vil.

"Right away Vanessa," I answered sarcastically low enough to get away with it.

"Did you go to that school telling them white folks you didn't get no rest due to the lights being off?"

The question instantly caused me to sweat. I knew the truth would get me crucified but lying wasn't an option because a question like that was only asked after facts had been obtained.

"Yes, ma'am," I mumbled dropping my head, "I just thought..."

I felt a sharp slap on the right side of my face.

"You don't have a thought, you think what I tell you to think, and you feel what I tell you to feel. What goes on in the house stays in this house do you understand me?"

"Yes, ma'am," I uttered as tears rolled down my face.

"Now get your hard-headed ass from out of my face!" she barked.

All night I thought about everything that took place that day, and I couldn't help but continue looping back around to what happened with Lamar. Lamar made me feel wanted and sexy. You know, like a woman. The next morning, I got up before the sun and stared in my closet waiting for the best outfit to jump out at me. After getting dressed I applied a little makeup and fluffed the ponytail on the side of my head. I made my way to the door, but not before being stopped by the tyrant.

"Where do you think you're going with the shit on your face?" Mother asked.

"I'm headed to school," I responded.

"Not looking like a dame clown you're not. You're too dark to be having that color make up on your face, stop trying to be white!"

I slid past her without saying a word. I wasn't going to let anything stop me from getting to school. I quickly washed my faced and darted out the door.

I arrived at school late, and the halls were already deserted. I briskly removed a piece of paper from my bag and wrote a little note. It read as follows: "I know you don't really know me but just wanted to let you know we live in the same apartment complex if you ever needed any sugar or anything." Signed Table Top. Looking around, I cautiously walked over to Lamar's locker and dropped the note in the slot. "If you ever need any sugar." Really Sam, I thought to myself as I heard the note hit the floor of his locker. Well, I couldn't take it back now. I hurried off upon hearing the bell that released the students from first period. The day drug as I watched the long hand slowly tick away on the clock. I wonder if he read the note? What if he and his friends are laughing at me? I couldn't stop thinking about the message I left. Ding-ding-ding, the bell sounded. I got my things and rushed out the door. When I got to my locker, there was a sticky note folded and tapped to the door. The note read: "I could always use sugar, here's my number." I went through the rest of the day scribbling Lamar and Sam surrounded by hearts on my notebook.

I stayed after that day for drill team practice. After changing out of my practice clothes, I went into the hallway to get a sip of water from the fountain. To my surprise, Lamar was coming out of his basketball sessions. He walked passed me but didn't say a word. I pretended not to notice.

"Table top," he called from halfway down the hall.

I stood up and wiped the water from my lips.

"Yeah," I called back.

"Come here for a second."

My heart started to race and before I knew it my feet were headed in his direction. My palms now sweating as they usually did when I was nervous, I kept walking toward him.

Upon reaching where he stood, he took me firmly by the hand and lead me to the custodial closet at the end of the hallway. Something told me he was no stranger to this closet. He cupped my booty and pulled me closer to him. I started to feel that tingle I felt back when I would hear mama moaning.

"I, I've never..." Barely getting my words out.

"I know," he stopped me midsentence while slowly unzipping his pants.

I wasn't sure what was getting ready to take place, but one thing was for certain, I was intrigued by how it made me feel. He placed his hands-on top of my head and guided me to my knees. Short of instruction, I grabbed his shaft that stood strongly at attention and wrapped my lips around the head of it. I looked up just as he tilted his head back. I didn't know exactly what I was doing but by the looks of the eyes rolling and lip biting I knew I was on the right path. His knees began to quiver with every stroke of my mouth, and without warning, I felt him thrusting in the back of my throat. He groaned like a lion in the wilderness, and it was like nothing I had heard before. Lacking restraint, he let out a foreign white substance that was now coming from my mouth.

"Damn girl, you sure you've never done that before?"

Challenging me while zipping up his pants.

Unsure as to what I had just done but I knew in that moment I felt needed, in control of his pleasure and completely on top of the world. He cleaned me up and walked out of the closet ahead of me.

"Call me later," he said with a look of satisfaction.

"Yeah, sure thing," I responded as I turned and walked in the opposite direction.

Walking out the doors of the school I was filled with reassurance. So, this is what it feels like to be the spider to the fly?

Chapter Two

There's Power In Numbers

Lying in bed staring blankly at the ceiling I was muddled by the fact that it had been three weeks since the closet escapade, and Lamar had been completely blowing me off. He barely even looked my way when we passed each other in the hall. Though things were estranged between us, I was heartened by the reality that I had been the apple of a few new eyes lately, and Lamar would soon be a distant memory of the past.

Nearly falling out of bed, I leaped up as "girls just want to have fun" came blazing through my cell phone speaker. Looking over at my alarm clock I noticed there was no time displayed on the screen. My phone continued to ring as I searched around my pillow looking to stop the obnoxious sound.

"Hello," I answered.

"Sam, where are you?" Kate said, "I'm at our meet-up spot."

"Sorry Kate, I was in a zone this morning. Go on without me, and I'll catch up with you at lunch."

Hanging up the phone, I got up and walked over to the light switch. I flipped the switch in the upward position confirming what I had already speculated, no electricity. The casino had taken possession of our light money per usual. Without further delay, I got dressed for school. On my way out the door, I stopped by the kitchen to grab a half eating sesame seed bagel I had left over from the day before. On the counter was a note written in mom's perfect penmanship. "Sam, no need to tell me about the lights because I already know and I'm working on it. I'll be home a little later. Come home straight after school, lock up the house, do homework and chores and find something for dinner. Text the cell if you need me, Mom." Sighing exasperatingly, I chucked the note into the garbage. If I need you huh? Yeah, I do need you, I need you to get these lights back on. I snarled as I continued towards the door.

The walk to school seemed to be never-ending. The sun was scorching hot and was showing my tattered jeans and wool sweater no mercy. Finally making it to the schoolyard, I headed towards the lunch area. As I approached the table, I removed my sweater and tied it loosely around my waist. I stood there for a moment allowing the sun to beat against the back of my chocolate skin. Out of the corner of my left eye, I could see the Alexander brothers watching me while I took my seat. Sam, Kate hissed in efforts to grab my attention.

"Thanks for standing me up this morning," Kate said, "You have to do better with setting your alarm."

"The alarm only works if there is power running to it," I explained in an annoyed tone.

"Oh, that again huh?" She said.

Ignoring her attempt to meddle, I quickly changed the subject.

"How long has the Alexander brothers been sitting over there?" I asked.

"Hadn't noticed," Kate replied looking over my shoulder to see them sitting directly behind us.

"Aye Sam, what's good?" One of the brothers asked.

I tilted my head slightly to the left, just enough to confirm the voice I had just heard.

"Nothing much Mike," I responded uninterestedly.

The Alexander brothers had a reputation around school for getting whatever they wanted at the expense of whomever they chose. Cute as they were, I wanted no parts of them. Overjoyed by the sound of the lunch bell I stood to my feet.

"I'll see you later Kate, I have a few things I need to get out of my locker."

"Sure thing, let's get together this afternoon," she suggested.

The last class came to an end, and my cell phone battery buzzed low charge. I was quickly reminded that there was no power at home, so I decided to head over to the park tucked away in the back of my apartment complex. Sitting on a bench taking in the crisp afternoon breeze, I noticed a group of kids in the distance. I kept my head down trying not to make eye contact when a familiar voice resonated from a far. I lifted my head to see Mike and two of his friends standing in front of me. Normally I would find any reason to dismiss myself from his presence, but this time was different. He had with him one of the smoothest guys I had ever met. The guy had broad shoulders, caramel complexion, athletic build, with a radiant smile and eye lashes that dang near curled up to his forehead. He wore a plain smoked grey jogging suit with a pair of white Nike's and judging by the way my nostrils did a dance; I was very pleased with whatever cologne he was rocking.

"Hey, Tate," I whispered like a bashful school girl.

"Hey Sam, is it cool if I sit down next to you?" He asked with a charming look on his face.

Without hesitation, I scooted over to make room for him to park all that deliciousness. It was no secret that I was indeed interested in picking up whatever he was lying down. Catching the vibes, the other two wandered not too far from where they began throwing the football.

Following small talk, Tate invited me to check out an abandoned apartment where he indicated all the kids hung out at after school. We snuck off trying not to bring any attention to ourselves.

We arrived at an apartment unit located on the bottom floor. Prior to checking for unlocked doors Tate opened the patio storage door and pulled me in. Me and closets had become real familiar with one another. Walking into the closet, the wanting's of my body started to make themselves known. The feeling of my pulsating labia's and the secretion that was now soaking my panties was a great indicator that my body was yearning for him. I could barely get the door closed before he grabbed me gently by the face and planted a wet one. I closed my eyes and took in the moistness of his upper lip. After what seemed to be only a brief second our lips unlocked, and I opened my eyes to see that smile I had come to like so much.

"Come on, let me show you something," he encouraged.

Walking up to the sliding glass door he slid a safety pin into the lock that he retrieved from his back pocket. You could tell he had done this a time or two and just like that the door was open. Looking back at me with enticing eyes, he invited me in. Though I was no newbie to adventure, I followed him dubiously.

Sure enough, the unit was indeed abandoned. It reeked of cat urine and trash that had been left from the previous renters. It was rather dusty and the only thing lighting the room was the sliver of sunlight coming through the tightly closed blinds. Fanning my nose, I continued with him to the master bedroom. The walls were marked with bed scuffing's, marker and tape residue. The carpet needed a serious cleaning. He walked in before me and laid the jacket of his jogging suit down on the carpet. He extended his hand as to offer me a moment in his space. With minor reservations, I embraced his offer. His hand now holding the rounded portion of my backside, I leaned into his clasp. Delicately laying me down my body was met with his. Moments into making out we heard the loud banter of the others. To my surprise, the boys had located us. They rushed in as Tate and I were sitting up.

"What's going on in here?" Asked Mike.

"Nothing," we both remarked together with a guilt-ridden look on our faces.

"So, you won't mind us joining then, right?"

I made my way to my knees in efforts to stand as Mike started towards us.

"Don't let the party end on our account," he teased.

"I was just getting ready to go," I stated in a flustered quaver.

The tension in the pit of my stomach began to intensify. Based on his sly grin and his fidgeting body, it was obvious he had something in mind, and it didn't involve me leaving. Trying to make light of an intense situation, I let out an awkward giggle. Standing in front of Tate and I, Mike kneeled and now was at eye level with me. My heart was pounding like a derby racehorse, and the sensations in my body moved from one of excitement and wonder too now terror. The feeling of control I usually got in these moments was nowhere to be felt. Seizing me by the neck, Mike began forcefully kissing my face and wandered down to my breast.

"Aye man, maybe you should stop," Tate firmly suggested.

Without saying a word, Mike looked at Tate with a stern countenance and continued slobbering on my neck.

"Come hold her arms," he commanded his friend.

A feeling of panic swept over me. Vacillating between whether to scream or comply, I laid there frozen. I focused in on a spot on the ceiling. The room started to spin, and I could feel the heat of his breath up against my cheek.

"Suck her breast!" He exhorted.

Nobody moved. Disappointed at his friend's reluctance to partake, he took a mouth full for himself. I cringed as he nibbled with aggression on the tip of my nipples. Still having said nothing, tears fell down my cheeks. All I could think about was the note mama left me to go straight home and lock up. Moving with much excitement, he tore apart the button on my pants. Things were moving faster than I could keep up with and before I could make sense of it, I felt a gut-wrenching penetration. Making eye contact with Tate who was holding me by the feet, I made a plea for help. Tate hung his head in guilt. It was clear that Mike was running the show, and no one was going to revolt against him, not even me.

After what seemed to be an eternity, God finally answered my cry. A key turned slowly in the doorknob. The boys jumped to their feet and hopped one by one out the bedroom window. Still processing what had just taken place I laid lifeless on the unpleasant smelling carpet. Oddly enough, at that moment the smelly carpet was my one piece of comfort. Strolling in like a night and shining armor came the maintenance man. He gasped when he encountered my half-naked body.

"Are you ok?" He asked. "Is it ok if I touch you?"

I began to weep. For the first time since the nightmare had begun, I could feel an emotion other than distress. Closing my shirt and instructing me to close my pants, he then wrapped me in his work vest which smelled of sweat and jalapenos. When I rose to my feet, there was an aching that radiated from my vaginal opening down my inner thighs and into my legs. I stumbled the first few steps eventually making my way to the buggy that was parked in front of the unit. Not before long the cart came to a halt in front of the office building of the apartment. My heart sunk into my stomach. Petrified by the unknown, I followed him into the manager's office.

"Have a seat," he advised, walking over to speak to the manager.

A marathon of thoughts overtook me. 'I was supposed to go straight home', 'I wasn't supposed to be in the empty apartment', 'I walked voluntarily into the building'.

"Sam," a soft female voice called out, bringing me back to reality, "Come into my office."

Barely having the strength to hold myself together I staggered to her office.

Hours had gone by, and we concluded it was best to inform mother of the situation, so she could make the decision of what was in my best interest. I dreaded the conversation, hell I dreaded even having to go home. I knew mother had given strict instructions and I deliberately disobeyed them. I made a plea to stay a little longer, but the office was getting ready to close and Jenny, the manager thought the sooner mama knew, the better. Walking like a prisoner on death row headed to execution, we finally made it to my front door. Standing there paralyzed, I stared at the door trying with everything in me to just disappear.

"Are you going to knock?" She asked.

I didn't say a word, nor did I budge. I heard a light knock on the door. I looked up to see that Jenny had beat me to it. Fear crushed me like a tidal wave, and before I knew it I was standing face to face with Goliath, the only difference is I was trembling and had no stones. Still saying nothing, I kept my head down.

"We had a situation take place today, may I come in to talk about it?" Jenny said.

I could hear the nervousness in her voice.

"Come in," mother agreed.

Never lifting my head from the ground, I could feel mama's eyes piercing through the top of my skull. Mother guided us to the guest living room and offered us a seat. This was only the second time my bottom graced the smooth leather of mama's couch, but this was the first time I wasn't going to get in trouble for it. Jenny did most of the talking while I sat there with tears rolling down my face. Mother's face was impassive, and it was very hard to read which way the pendulum was swinging. When Jenny was done, she looked down at me and inquired if I had anything else to add. I silently shook my head, never lifting it from its downward position. Before being escorted out, Jenny turned to mama and made one last recommendation.

"This is tough for us all, but I urge you to consider getting some counseling for her, I think it would be helpful."

Feeling irritated that this woman was already in her home, mother continued to show her out the door. The door shut, and it felt like an avalanche was coming down Mount Everest. Not only were my palms sweating but my armpits had joined the party and brought along with them my forehead. Sweat seemed to be pouring out of me like a faucet.

"I leave to go to work, and you're out here being hot," mama insinuated.

"Hot" was a word mama used to describe an adolescent girl who acts much older than she is by way of dressing, behavior presentation or quick to engage in sexual activities.

"Look at me when I'm talking to you!" She ordered.

Slowly raising my head, I struggled to make eye contact.

"I should whoop your ass for being outside when I clearly told you to come straight home!" She snapped. "Go to your room!"

I wasted not another minute; I practically ran to my room.

"This wouldn't have happened if you weren't out there being fast!" Another one of mom's whore like references.

Shutting my door, I fell to my knees. I felt tainted and damaged but more than anything I felt empty. The buildup of emotions started to wail up in my throat. There was now a lump of anxiety making its way up my neck. My heart physically hurting from the pressure of what I was feeling, I was almost sure I was getting ready to have a heart

27

attack. I rushed to my bed, put my face into my pillow and let out a scream and then another one and then another. Feeling somewhat of a release, I laid there in disarray and thought to myself... 'Why couldn't she love me at that moment?' 'Why was I not good enough to be held?' 'I don't deserve protection.' 'I'm not worthy of setting boundaries.'

Maybe mama was right; it was my fault. You can't put yourself in these situations and expect your no to hold value. A multitude of feelings and thoughts continued to bombard my mind. I crawled into the fetal position, rocking myself to sleep until I finally fell into a deep slumber.

Chapter Three

She Gets It Honest

"Daddy, I'll be back later!" I yelled while heading to the door.

I could hear my girl's music bumping all the way up the driveway. We were getting ready to hit the strip, and when we got together, it was a guaranteed good time.

"I see you looking all delicious," Courtney complimented as I opened the passenger car door. She continued. "Give me a twirl and show me what you're working with."

I smiled as big as the sun as I turned in a circle showing off my neon stripped crop top sitting over my sun-kissed navel and my white shorts that stopped right above the bottom of my cheeks.

"Are these shorts fly or what? I asked.

"Like a bird on a sunny day," she remarked with a nod of approval.

Courtney and I had met a few months after I moved down here to stay with my dad and have been inseparable since. After the gang rape back home, I spiraled out of control. My behavior was off the charts, my lack of respecting authorities reached an all-time high, and I became a habitual thief, stealing any and everything I could get my hands on. It was only a matter of time before I had to stay with my dad. Mama and I were on the verge of killing each other, figuratively speaking of course. Being at daddies was a breath of fresh air. He and I had always been close, more like friends than father-daughter. Daddy understood my free spirit, and he allowed me to spread my wings like the beautiful butterfly that I was. Though he allowed me to be me, there was one thing we had in common, and that was our fire like personality. We were both extremely stubborn, and that was to our detriment at times.

During my short time in The Bay Area, I had already been through one cheating boyfriend and one failed workplace romance. I decided I just wanted to focus on me and my girls, so when I wasn't working I was living it up with Sasha or Courtney. While I had already dabbled in a little bit of the streets, I was getting ready to be introduced to a whole other side of it.

"Did you bring the good stuff?" Courtney asked while letting down the top of her new wine-colored mustang.

"You know I did," I stated as I held up the bottle of Vodka.

I wasn't big on drinking, I had what the girls considered a natural high, but Courtney tended to loosen up once she had a drink or two.

"Girl, you aren't tired of making nickels working at that fast food joint yet?" Court blurted out as I finished taking the rest of the party favors out of my bag.

I guess I hadn't thought about it. I had been at Pasta Pizzazz for some time now, and it seems to be paying enough for me to do what I needed to do.

"You got something better," I asked as I began to light up the blunt.

"You know big sis will always look out for you, don't trip."

Uncertain by what she meant by that I turned up the music and took one more puff before passing along the joint.

It had reached nightfall when we pulled up to the driveway of my father's house.

"See you later sis," I expressed turning to get out of the car.

Before I could get both legs out, I felt a smack on my backside.

"Next week I'm going to take you to one of my homeboy's parties," she said, "It's for grown folks, but I can get you in."

Not sure what to make of the smack on my ass, I simply nodded, shut the door and made my way up the driveway. As I approached the door, I could hear daddy yelling. I pulled my key out and inserted it in the keyhole. Before I could turn the nob, the door flung open, and one of my younger sisters came rushing out in tears. I entered with caution looking at the surroundings. It looked as though Hurricane Katrina had made a visit to our living room sparing no furniture. I could see my stepmother on the edge

32

of the couch holding her face crying. I finally made it to my father who was cooling down in the garage.

"What happened tonight daddy?" I inquired plopping myself down on the chair beside him.

"I'm tired of these hoes," he said, "All these bitches do is disrespect me and leach off their mother and me. I'm sick of it!"

This was daddies usual rant, and though it had some validity, it usually stemmed from daddy's lack of control.

"Ok daddy, take a moment to breathe and then get some rest," I advised as I hugged him and headed back into the house.

I stopped and took one more look at my stepmother. Though my heart broke for her, my dad was my everything, and my alliance was always with him. I carried on to my bedroom closing my door and embracing the peace that filled the room. It had been a long night.

"Sam... Sam... wake up," my sister nagged, "Can I borrow your shirt?"

"Go ahead but don't bring it back musty or dirty," I replied opening one eye.

My sister hopped off my bed with excitement and headed towards the door clutching my off the shoulder black and pink Baby Phat shirt. Always asking to wear my stuff, I mumbled as I closed my eyes. Before I could fall back to sleep, my alarm clock went off. 'Shake it like a salt shaker' the alarm continued to blare. Sitting up slowly, I stretched and placed both feet on the floor. Today was the day Courtney was taking me to my first adult party, and I was low key nervous. After hopping in the shower, I put on my cutest turquoise laced panty and bra set, then packed a bag. Anticipating what the night could entail, I packed a little of everything and waited in suspense for Courtney's arrival.

It wasn't long after I heard a hunk sound from out front. As I approached the car I noticed she had already scooped Sasha, the liquor was flowing, and the bud had been lit.

"Are you guys crazy?" I asked as I fanned the smoke coming out of the driver's window. "Are ya'll trying to get me killed?"

"Shut up and get your fine ass in the car," Courtney remarked rolling up her window.

Court had a habit of make sexual comments to me, and I just went along with it. I jumped in the back and instantly reached for the happy grass. I didn't know what to expect, but I knew I needed my nerves to be calm for whatever took place.

After what seemed to be a short distance we pulled up to a grey one-story house that appeared to only have two windows max. When we got to the door Court, and Sasha hugged the guy standing outside and introduced me as their little sister. He looked me up and down and gave the ok for us all to enter. Sasha looked back at me, winked and proceeded into the house. Upon entering I noticed it was packed wall to wall, the air was dense, and just about every girl was half dressed and tooted over in front of a guy. The girls led me to a back room where they began disrobing. Confused by the change of outfits I watched attentively but said nothing.

"Tonight, you grow up, tonight you gain your independence," Courtney commented.

Still processing exactly what was going on, I swallowed a gulp of the vodka that sat next to me and followed suit. When we were done changing, Sasha yelled,

"It's showtime!" and without further ado, she left the room heading back out into the party. She found the DJ, whispered in his ear and the music changed instantly. Court made her way through the crowd and joined Sasha.

"We brought someone special tonight," Courtney demanded, "She's our little sister so be nice."

Almost in shock, my knees chattered like teeth on a winter New York morning. I didn't know what I was embarking upon, but I knew it involved all these people and myself.

Standing there like a deer in the headlights, Court and Sasha began to dance around me, touching themselves and each other. Anxiety now rising in the pit of my stomach like gas after a double beef spicy burrito, I became frantic. Before I could even take a deep breath, I took off running back towards the room. I stood behind the door watching as Sasha and Courtney commanded the room and money fell like snowflakes in Winter Wonder Land. The money was coming quick and easy, and they weren't even working hard. I could do that, I thought to myself.

Right as the song came to an end, a shadow appeared in front of me. Looking up I saw a tall chocolate brother, with gym grown pecs and biceps and dreads that hung past the middle of the toned arch in his back. His lips were very pronounced and his eyebrows extremely thick.

"Why are you hiding behind the door lil' bit?" He asked with a look of curiosity.

"Who said anything about hiding," I answered with an attitude, "Besides the party is out there so why are you even back here asking what I'm doing?" I continued sarcastically.

He laughed and offered me a drink, and after a few of them, he was looking more and more appetizing.

"You here with someone?" I asked him.

"And if I am?" he replied as he scooted closer to me.

"I mean, I don't want no problems."

He then leaned in and pressed his luscious lips against mine mid-sentence. Our lips melted into each other, and at that point, I had ninety-nine problems and whoever he came with wasn't one of them. He took me by the shoulders and laid me back licking me from my neck all the way to my inner thigh. I grabbed his face and held it right there in position as I wrapped both legs around his neck. Moving my panties over with his teeth he wasted no time diving in; I let out a moan. He had just begun round two when Sasha and Court busted through the door. It startled me, but he didn't even budge. It was as if this was normal at these parties. I laid there a little embarrassed as the girls got their things.

"Toby, can you take her home?" Court asked.

"Yeah, I got her," Toby answered never taking his face from between my legs.

"No thanks," I said, "I want to go home with you guys," I butted in sliding up the bed.

I gathered my things and stood next to the girls, only they didn't move. They both stood oddly staring at Toby.

"Alright man," Court said.

"Alright," he said while extending $60 in my direction.

I looked at the money, and then at them.

"Don't be stupid girl, take your money," Court commanded.

I wasn't sure what the money was for, I mean he ate me out why did he have to pay. I apprehensively took the money and followed the girls out.

Weeks had passed since the awkward experience at the party, but I couldn't help but to think about how easily the money came. Court had been reaching out, but I picked up a few extra shifts in efforts of avoiding her. She didn't necessarily do anything wrong, but I was confused by what I felt. I liked it more than I wanted to give credit for. After a long shift, I finally clocked out and went home. When I got there, I could tell daddy was in one of his moods. He started with me as soon as I walked in the door.

"Where were you?" He said.

"At work daddy!"

"All night?" He went on.

"Yes, all night," I answered irritably.

I went to walk away when I felt a bottle hit me in the back. I threw the keychain I had dangling from my wrist at his face, and before I knew it, we were tussling. He lifted me up by the throat and slammed me into the wall. I started to feel a shortage of oxygen, and there was a shift in my vision. In the distance, I could hear what sounded like a faint plea from my stepmother for him to let me go. I mustered up the last bit of strength I had and kneed him right where the sun doesn't shine. He threw me on the bed, and I hit the floor gasping for whatever bit of air I could take in. Daddy and I had been in many scuffles but never had he manhandled me in that manner. I picked up the phone and petitioned for Courtney to come get me.

I stayed over at Courtney's for a while, but this stay was a little different from other times I stayed the night. This visit, Court stated I had to decide if I was in or out, and by in, she meant withholding nothing. That night, Courtney made love to me in a way I had never experienced. The way she caressed me, the way she passionately kissed and gently rubbed me down. She connected with me in a way emotionally I had never encountered. I laid in bed staring at the ceiling listening as she promised to always look out for me and vowed that if I rolled with her, I would always have my own, wanting for nothing. It was in that moment the message I received as a young girl was solidified. My body was powerful and held the key to getting whatever it was my heart sought after, and I intended to use it for such.

As time went on, I went to more and more parties. Some parties I would just dance, some I would provide sexual services and others I would just watch, but at every

40

party what took place was my choice. However, being taught the game came with a price and Court made sure to collect her cut. I had to say I enjoyed rolling side by side with my big sisters and before I knew it, I was all in.

My grades began to slip in school because let's face it, between parties, home instabilities and my actual job I was getting no sleep. I didn't want to let go of Pasta Pizzazz and raise red flags about where all the money was coming from, and I wasn't ready to give up my partying life, so I continued with them all in hopes that I wouldn't crash and burn and for a while I didn't.

Though money was coming, and my girls and I were straight, I still longed for something more, and something was missing. I thought maybe if I screwed for free, I would start to feel something I hadn't yet felt. I screwed around from my boss to my teacher, yet nothing seemed to satisfy this craving I had a deeper connection.

I stumbled through high school finally getting my diploma and things at home seemed to have intensified. Things weren't the same as they were when I had first come to stay with daddy, and it was evident that our tempers were ticking time bombs waiting to see who's would go off first. I stayed a few weeks past graduation, but eventually, I knew my time in the Sunshine state had come to a dead-end. My older sister from my mom reached out to me and offered to let me come stay with her. I had been away from Washington for years, but I was a new Sam, and I wasn't sure the Evergreen state was ready for me, but one thing was certain, I was ready for it.

Poem
She's Tired

His love wrapped around her neck penetrating her innermost being.

Tainting the depths of her soul while whispering his fantasies.

His bone now of her bone and his flesh of her flesh, aborting her innocence and leaving her in a pile of nothingness.

His sex demon now intertwined with hers, obeying his command is a must, she's a modern-day Jezebel feeding his raging lust, but she's tired….

Ripped apart piece by piece she gradually starts to deteriorate.

Her body being devoured, and her heart ate off a broken plate.

A different star spreading her sky as the moon watches in pleasure. A sex object to them all, she conforms to withstand any weather, but she's tired…

Wrapping herself up inside the sheets, like a caterpillar in a cocoon. She slowly dies in hopes that new life will come soon.

The wind speaks of a well where it has been said she could find rest. Seeking the sun for her midnight hour she packs a bag of self-loath, shame and lust.

On her journey to the land of identity, she sold her self-esteem along the way, sitting at the table with lions, on her insecurity playground she allowed them to play.

A wise man once said love is patient, so she waits, but she's tired

Chapter Four

Lullaby

"Ugh, it's raining again!" I complained staring off the balcony of our second story apartment.

"Yes girl," Kendra replied while stepping out to join me, "Don't act like you forgot how much it rains here.

"I guess I just got so used to the sunshine back in the Bay."

"I know you miss it," she said. "But this is home now so get used to it," Kendra joked as she gave me a shove in my shoulder.

"I guess she was right," I responded.

I missed my girls back in California, but this was home now, so I'd better gather an umbrella, a pair of rain boots and get familiar with the nearest Starbucks. I got to get to work, get out and see some old friends; my sister suggested as she headed out the door. Old friends huh, that wasn't such a bad idea, and I really could use some time out of the house.

I eagerly picked up my phone; I knew exactly who to call. After a few rings, I heard a soft voice come from the other end.

"Hey Kailey, how are you?" It's Sam.

"Hey, Sam," Kailey responded. "I heard you were back in town, can't wait to see you."

After a long overdue conversation, we decided it would be best to link up, and what better place for two young ladies than the mall? I threw on my Nike sweats and Ugg boots and made my way to the bus stop. The rain had begun to let up some but not enough to spare me from looking like a wet puppy. When I arrived at the mall, Kailey was already there holding two mango bubble teas.

"I guess some things never changed," I said smiling with appreciation.

We sat at a table in the middle of the food court and continued to catch up. After what seem to be hours of banter, Kailey informed me that she met a girl at the transit on her way here who had invited her to church and she extended the invitation to me. With some reservation, I accepted the invitation. It had been some time since I had gone to church and truth be told I was silently praying God didn't strike me down upon reentry.

Accepting Kailey's invite to church had been on my mind for days, and I tried to come up with every excuse imaginable not to attend, but in the end, I decided to join her. The service was long as excepted and in the left corner, third pew from the back sat a short young man wearing black Jordan's and a fitted cap who stared in our direction all during service. Annoyed by the number of times he licked his lips I lifted my fan and blocked my face. When church was over, we were approached by Mr. Lick-a-lot and the young lady whom Kailey had met earlier in the week. He was introduced as Darnell, and her name was Latonya. Following our quick chat, we decided to hang outside of church. I was returning to the state and could use all the friends I could get at this point.

We hung together day in and day out for months and I must say, things were cool in the beginning. At about month three I noticed Kailey start to talk about Darnell quite a bit. I didn't see why she was interested in him. She was two times his height, his clothes drowned him, and puberty

47

was not on his side. I tried to convince her she could do better, but she was fixated on him and because she was my friend I just wanted her happy, the only problem was he and Latonya were in a confusing on and off again relationship. Latonya took a strong liking to Kailey but was really dry towards me. I couldn't figure out why being that I was on my (Good Sam behavior), but after a while the why became irrelevant and the (Bad Sam) came to play.

Sitting around one evening after choir rehearsal, Latonya leaned over and whispered.

"You think you're all that because you have a big booty and can sing," she said. "You get everything, but I have something you will never get."

"And what's that?" I asked, amused by her statement.

"Darnell!" She voiced in an intimidating tone.

I rolled my eyes in disappointment that I was even entertaining the conversation, I shifted my body and continued sitting pretty. I would be lying if I said her last comment didn't get to me. Did she really think I couldn't get Darnell? Did she truly believe he was untouchable? Now feeling challenged, I felt the spirit of seduction come over me. I know my girl Kailey was super interested in him, but I had peeped that he was more interested in me and though I was so out of his league I couldn't dare let Latonya think she had one up on me. So, I batted my eyelashes, bit my bottom lip and gave my hips a twist in Darnell's direction. Noticing he was alone, I slid up against him and asked if he wanted to chill, just the two of us and to no surprise he accepted. You see, I didn't know much about a lot but one thing I knew how to do was bait a man. Rolling my eyes as I walked away, I knew it wouldn't take much to have shorty swing my way.

When he came over to hang out things were awkward between us. It was very clear that I wasn't interested in him like he was interested in me. It was hard for me to fake it but all I could think about was Latonya's comment and though Kailey stated she didn't care that he and I were talking, I knew this was going to throw a wrench in our relationship. Sitting across from him I kept asking myself if proving Latonya wrong was worth all of this? Then I saw her in the back of my mind sitting with such assurance that she had Darnell on lock and it gave me just enough push to go ahead and entertain his presence.

As time went on, I continued to dodge his calls and duck his visits, but I could see he was slowly straggling back to Latonya. I knew it was only a matter of time before my cold demeanor would be felt and he would start to stray, so I did what I knew how to do best. I broke him off some of this smooth chocolate bunny and as excepted his nose was wide open. I won't even front, shorty was working with something serious and that alone kept us between the sheets often for months.

I started to realize that though Darnell wasn't my type he was a great friend. We had a ton of laughs and did a lot of fun stuff together but that all came to a halt when it came time to cash in the check for all the unprotected sex we had been having. Brushing my teeth getting ready for work, I started to gag and before I knew it, I was vomiting. Oddly enough I had been feeling nauseous for days now. Not sure what to make of it, I checked my calendar only to realize I was three days late for my menstrual. That was odd being my cycle came like clockwork. I called into work and walked to the nearest Walgreens drug store making sure to grab two pregnancy tests just to be on the safe side. Wish I had been on top of things with buying condoms, I thought humoring myself. When I arrived back to the house, I sat on the couch trying to wrap my mind around what I was going to do if the tests were positive or if I would be willing to give up the 'mandingo' if they were negative. I guess the only thing left to do was to take the test. I walked calmly into the bathroom and closed the door. After five minutes passed, I looked at both tests, both which confirmed pregnancy. I began to weep. I didn't even like him like that; we weren't even in what I considered an actual relationship. He isn't ready to be a father; my mind was perplexed. I went to my room and cried myself to sleep.

Woken up by a loud growl coming from my stomach, I sat up and looked over at the clock. I must have slept the day away because it was now 10:00 pm. I looked at my phone to find several missed calls and messages from Darnell. I had forgotten we had a meeting in the bedroom schedule for tonight, but at this point that was the last thing on my mind. I laid back down trying to figure out how I was going to tell him the news about the baby. I took a deep breath and realized there was no way to tell him other than just tell him. I picked up the phone and slowly dialed his number. Darnell picked up almost immediately.

"Where have you been girl?" He said. "Are you hiding from daddy?" He asked pompously.

Nearly vomiting at his last statement, I took another deep breath, swallowed and then begin to speak hesitantly.

"We're pregnant," I said softly.

His silence spoke louder than any words ever could at that moment.

"Darnell!" I shouted.

"What?" He asked confused. "So, what are you going to do?" His voice now moving from arrogance to uncertainty.

"What am I going to do?" He replied.

Was he serious? Did I get myself pregnant?

"Sam, what are you going to do?" He continued. "Are you going to get an abortion?" He barked, bringing me back to reality.

"No, no I'm not, and if you don't want to help out, then that's fine," I said, "I'll take care of this baby alone but once you make the decision to walk away then consider this our last conversation."

"Yep," he countered in the most confident tone I heard from him since I told him the news.

"Ok," I stated and hung up the phone.

At that moment, it was very clear to me that this was a journey I was going to have to embark on alone and surprisingly I was at peace. I laid back down rubbing my belly.

"I guess it's just you and me," I whispered to the gift growing inside me.

I was going to love this child and he or she was going to love me back unconditionally, I was sure of it.

It wasn't long before word got out that I was pregnant. By this time, I was very active at the church we all attended, and the news spread like wildfire. I started getting calls and messages from every end but especially from Latonya. I recalled that Latonya and Darnell were on and off for years, and though they were off when I got pregnant, Latonya always thought they would have a baby and be a family. Little did she know at this moment I wish it were her and not me.

It was about a month since I had informed Darnell about the baby and the news started to die down. We were sitting in church watching the clock as we usually did when one of the co-Pastors brought the word when I noticed Latonya slumped over in the pew behind me. She appeared lethargic as if she had the flu and had been up all night. When church was over, the First Lady rushed her to the hospital. We all waited in anticipation hoping all was well and when we received the news it was more than any of us expected, Latonya was pregnant, and the baby was Darnell's. My mouth fell to the floor in disbelief. What was she thinking? Had the competition for Darnell gotten that serious? I mean I guess it was her man first but why now? I had so many questions and so little answers. The buzz picked up again and all three of us were now at the center of it.

With everything that had been going on over the last few months, I kept my head buried in work and ministry stuff. Darnell and I did not speak one word to each other until I found out I was pregnant with a boy. I let him know he was having a son and we did not speak again until the day I gave birth. Of course, I heard from Latonya here and there and she too had a son exactly one month and two days after me. This whole situation was a huge mess, but it brought forth two blessings.

During the pregnancy, I had to move out of where I was staying, and I had no family to stay with. One of the elders from the church took me in and helped me figure out this single mom life I had undertaken. As I thought I was prepared to raise this baby alone, it was difficult, and I was tired. I loved my son but not having his father around to help really hurt. Everything was starting to take a toll on me and it was noticed by all. One Thursday after choir rehearsal I was standing outside taking in the cool night air when I felt a tap on my lower back from the choir director. He took a moment to encourage me, then smiled and turned to walk away. It was nice because though I had support from others, a breath of fresh air was truly needed. He was motivating, uplifting and he made sure to be a constant encouraging mentor for me in the months that followed. We spent a lot of time in communication, things were finally starting to look up and for once it looked as though the smoke was clearing.

Chapter Five

Preying Hands

"Aunty come get Elliot I'm heading out," I called from across the hall.

Elliot was now three months old, and it hadn't yet hit me that I was a mother. I had moved out from the Elder and moved in with Aunt Dorian who helped me a lot with my son. She kept Elliot, so I could hang with my friends and live what I thought was a normal 19-year-old life. I loved going to the mall and the movies, but the real fun happened at night. You know that bottle popping, booty tossing dance to your feet hurt kind of fun. Being a mom was cool and all, but none of my other friends had children. They were able to come and go as they pleased and thanks to Aunt D, so was I.

A few things had changed since I had my baby boy but not much. I had recently reconnected with some old friends, the Davidson's that over the years became family. I met them when we first relocated to Seattle. They had a dance ministry and a heart for the youth. During that time, I was going through a lot, and they had become like parents to me. Teaching me the gospel of Jesus and showing me what a healthy African American family looked like. Everything I experienced with them was very new in my world. They took me to concerts, church, dinner and poured into me. I lost contact with them when I left to stay with my dad but was happy to have them back into life.

Lori and her husband Reverend Mitch Davidson had children way younger than me who I considered little brother and sisters, they were truly God sent and I had nothing but the utmost respect for them. Lori had been through a lot with me. She even took me to counseling after the situation in that abandoned apartment. Being around them brought back so many memories, it was like old times. They were doing some ministry out of their home, and I was excited to be apart. They lived and breathed outreach, and though I was still trying to figure my place in the world of religion, I knew I loved what I felt when we worshipped.

I attended their vocal rehearsals on Monday, Bible study on Wednesday and over for dinner, counseling and anything else that came up. Lori and Mitch even started getting involved with Elliot. They had become another strong support system for me, and I loved it. They were very familiar with my past and were committed to helping me grow and what they called heal. They said that God had something better for me and that I was fearfully and wonderfully made, whatever that meant.

The more I hung out with them, the more I started to change. Lori explained to me that I should be more modest. She said that Christian young ladies should not wear clothing that was so tight and revealing. She went on to say that because my body was shaped so nicely, I had to be more careful about what I wore. I didn't know why she harped on my clothing so much. I wore the latest fashion as did any girl my age, skinny jeans and leggings. But because I respected her opinion, I obeyed.

During the night of bible study, I arrived at the Davidsons house early and let myself in as I always did. I could hear Reverend Mitch screaming and cursing at Lori. I had never heard him so angry or use such implicit choice words. I sat down on the couch and waited until I heard silence.

"Hello, I'm here," I called out but no response. I called out again, "Hello!"

I heard a door close and then footsteps on the stairs.

"Hey Sam, you're early," Rev Mitch pointed out.

"Yeah, I was in the area after work and thought I'd just come now. Hope that's ok?"

"That's quite alright," he encouraged.

Looking over his shoulder, I could see Lori shuffling towards us. She looked depleted and uninterested in sharing the same space with anyone. However, she carried on into the living area with a half-cocked smile and the warmest greeting she could conjure up. Something was off, and I was getting ready to inquire when we heard a knock at the door. The others were here, and I realized it wasn't the right time to engage in what was going on.

Bible study went well, and I stuck around after the others departed to talk with Lori and Mitch for a little. They always had some nuggets of wisdom to impart or a word of prayer to offer. I sat on the stairs picking their brain about something I was considering when Rev Mitch asked me about my dating life. I had been talking to someone, but it was in no way serious. Heck, I wasn't even sure if we were considered dating. I brushed off the question with a joke and continued talking about this ministry move I was considering. Rev Mitch interpreted again this time inquiring about how I like to be handled in the bedroom. Completely taken back by his question, I just stared awkwardly.

"I would like to pick you up and take you up these stairs," he continued squinting his eyes and scrunching his face up in efforts of looking sexy.

"Mitch!" Lori yelled, "That's totally inappropriate!"

"I'm only joking with her women, she knows I'm playing," he snapped looking back at her.

Things were getting weird, and I figured this was the perfect time to make my exit. Well, it's getting late and I should get home to my son. I'll catch up with you guys later; I announced as I stood up and a gathered my things.

I didn't sleep well that night. Mitch's comments played back in my mind. He had a pattern in the past of saying things that were a bit inappropriate as well as looking at you in a way as to undress you with his eyes but never was he so straightforward about it or in front of Lori. I didn't know quite what to make of it. I went over the scenario many times wondering if I gave off any indication that I was into him like that. I had been told before that I have a seductive personality and in times where I thought I was friendly, it was in fact coming off flirtatious but nothing about my behavior tonight visibly stood out, so I let it go.

It had been two weeks since the ordeal at bible study, and I had not heard from the Davidsons. That was until this afternoon. I was at work on my lunch break when I received a call from Mitch. Mitch explained that he, Lori and the kids were having a little BBQ for dinner and wanted Kailey, Elliot and I to join them. Kailey and I became roommates a few weeks ago, and we did everything together. Kailey had known the Davidsons as long as I had, and it wasn't unusual for them to invite her to the places in which they invited me. I agreed with us going over for dinner and went back to work to let Kailey know. She regretfully informed me that she wouldn't be able to come due to a prior engagement, so I decided to go on without her. I figured Lori could help out

with Elliot.

Work had finally come to an end, and though I was tired I wanted to keep to my word and at least stop by. When I got to their house, I noticed one of the cars were gone, thinking nothing of it I grabbed the baby out of the backseat and continued to the front door. I knocked and received no answer. I knocked again only this time I twisted the doorknob as well. The door opened, and I let myself in. I saw Mitch on the back-porch grilling. I placed Elliot down on the couch to finish his nap and proceeded towards the back-sliding door.

"Where's Lori?" I inquired stepping out onto the smoky porch.

"Oh, she's not here," he replied closing the grill.

Confused as to whether he meant not now or not at all I started to feel tense. Something about this wasn't sitting right with me, so I got up and walked back into the house.

"Where are the kids?" I asked.

"Out," he answered almost excitingly.

I walked to the kitchen to grab a glass of water. I wasn't good at handling situations of pressure. I tended to freeze up when I was in predicaments that cause a need for me to speak out, speak up for or defend myself. For years as a child, my mother would tell me, "You don't have a thought, you think what I tell you to think, and you feel what I tell you to feel." That way of thinking manifested itself in how I showed up in sticky situations as an adult. I felt silenced, and I tended to conform to whatever the adult or person of authority was inflicting. When it came to me standing up against my oppressors, I simply went along to get along.

Leaning up against the counter trying to catch my breath I felt his body press up against the back of mine. I gasped and closed my eyes. Why was he doing this? Did I ask for it? Could I say no? I couldn't decide whether to run away or push him off me. So, I stood there with my eyes closed hoping at that moment I would transport elsewhere. I felt his arm reach around my hip cupping my vagina with his right-hand. I gasped again, this time so loudly it could be heard a mile away.

"Please don't," I uttered, never opening my eyes.

"Shhh," he commanded.

I had been in several situations, but this one felt different. I had so much respect for this man, and I thought he loved me in a way that didn't require me to give him me sexually. That is what I loved about him the most. His hand was now rubbing in an upward motion between my legs, I trembled. Wrapping his left hand around the other side of my waist, he brought his right hand up to assist in unbuttoning my pants. I grabbed on to the counter for dear life. This was actually happening. Say something dammit, I screamed on the inside, yet nothing came out. It was either fight or flight, and at that moment, I was on the first thing smoking up out of there, that is mentally of course.

"Please don't," I begged again.

He had already started pulling down my pants and kissing on the back of my neck. Pressing all 300 lbs. up against my 145 lb. build, with his mouth near the back of my ear.

"You like that?" he whispered.

It was almost as if he wasn't himself. He had reached a point of no return.

"You don't want to do this, think about Lori," I urged.

Before I could say another word, I felt his penis kiss the opening of my vaginal lips. Bracing myself for the impact of penetration, I shriveled up as to crawl inside myself but after a few seconds had gone by, I felt nothing. He tried entering me several times but was unable to perform, and just when I thought I had made it out unscathed, I felt a horrific piercing between my legs. He placed his left hand on my back and arched me further into the counter. It was as if I was now having an out of body experience. I realized he had jammed his fingers inside me and the pain I felt was the scrapping of my insides. Yet even still I didn't fight, nor did I scream. I lifted my head and looked out the kitchen opening at my son sleeping peacefully on the couch. With ever forceful blow all I could do is draw from the peace my son was letting off.

The nightmare finally came to an end. He took his fingers out of me, and I hurried to pull up my pants. Slowly turning around never looking him directly in his eyes I could see him smiling with contentment out of my peripheral, steadily licking my secretion off his fingers. I cringed inside. I kept my head down, grabbed my sons bottle off the counter and walked in the direction of where Elliot was resting. Mitch placed his arm in front of me causing me to drop the bottle.

"Was it good, did you like it?" He asked seemingly proud of what he had just done.

Was this even a real question, I thought to myself. Saying nothing I walked with urgency over to my baby boy who had slept through that entire horror. I did not make any other stops; I headed straight for the door.

"This will stay between us, right?" He asked stopping me right before I exited.

"Yes," I quickly answered wanting nothing more than to get out the door.

"Good because this would hurt Lori," he said.

Staring at down at my baby I nodded in agreeance. He stepped away from the door, and I walked as fast as my legs would carry me. I was mortified.

Upon reaching home, I was greeted at the door by Kailey.

"How was the food?" She asked oblivious to the fact that I was the meal that had been served up.

I handed her the baby and went straight to the shower. I turned the water to scorching hot, yet I couldn't scrub the feeling of him off. I sat in the shower watching the water run down the drain, wishing I could wash away the mental stain. Mitch had taught me so much in the time I knew him but what I learned today rung familiar, and that was that love hurts. I got out of the shower feeling just as dirty as I felt when I got in. My insides pulsating from the trauma I had just endured. I flopped on my bed trying to soak in the events that took place. You did this to yourself Sam. How could you be so stupid? You can't put yourself in these situations. I continued to beat myself up. This hadn't been my first time at the rodeo so maybe I was bringing this on myself. I laid in bed still in shock. My mind was so all over the place. In need of a release, I took a razor from underneath my pillow and placed it on my wrist. Before I could lay into my skin my phone started vibrating and Roy, the choir directors name flashed across the screen. I let out a sigh. Though I was happy to see him calling, I needed everything this cut had to offer. I closed my eyes and sliced into my wrist, and for the first time I felt something other than helplessness.

Poem

I Am

I am

A blank canvas painted on by dirty brushes

A mixture of black clouds, unclean hands and jail house lunches

I am

A filthy rag washed up by the noon day tide

A star that's lost it shine and the cheapest of all the wines

I am

Masters property my worth is found in him

Navigating life like a rock not yet polished into a gem

I am

Coffee on a cold winter morning and a blanket to keep you warm

A ship that's lost its sail and washed out to sea during a storm

I am

Ready for change, to evolve and become someone new

I am who I will be because I am a reflection of you

I am Becoming..

Chapter Six

The Fall

"You like it when I go deep don't you, who's is it?"

"Yours daddy," I groaned as I indulged in every bit of his strokes.

Legs spread like an eagle from the dashboard to the steering wheel, steaming up the windows as we partook in one another's gift. Arching my back as to allow him access deeper into my ocean, he swam freely backstroking on the waves of my walls. Only to drown in a puddle of my love juices, he clasped in gratification.

We had been together a while now, and car sex seemed to be a daily for Roy and me. Yes, I was officially dating the choir director. In the beginning, I wondered why we had to meet in secret locations and only had sex in the car. He told me that it was more fun that way and that he wanted to make sure I really loved him before we went public. He went on to explain that he had been hurt badly in the past and he couldn't take another heartbreak. I asked him if me being 19 and him being 47 had something to do with it; he reassured me that wasn't the case. To be honest, I didn't care at this point, all I knew was that we had some of the best sex. Roy and I became romantically involved shortly after the attack by Mitch. He was there for me in more ways than I ever could ask. He was so sweet and charming; there was something about him that I couldn't get enough of. We spent so much time together, the more we engaged the more I fell in love with him.

"Meet me at the trail in 30 minutes and wear those purple silk panties I like," he requested right before hanging up the phone.

Roy was fluent in impromptu sex gatherings, and I got excited every time. When I got to the trail, Roy was parked at the farthest end of the parking lot with his headlights turned off. Upon reaching the car, he got out and instructed me to put my hands on the hood. Loving where this was going, I did so enthusiastically. Sliding his hand up my skirt I tilted my head back and licked my lips. Seductively moving my panties to one side, he entered me desirously. Ah, I inhaled taking in the beast of his of body.

Roy had such a way with me. He made me feel like I was the most important person in the world and I never wanted to leave his presence. After we were done, we sat in the car and laughed for hours. He inquired about school, work, and Elliot. He always encouraged me to be all that I could be, he was like nobody I had ever dated, and I was on top of the world with him.

"When do you expect you'd be ready to meet my family?" I asked curiously.

"Soon," he said, which always seemed to be his answer.

We had been together going on two and half years, and we were still on the down low.

"Are you playing me or something?" I teased. "Do you have a chick on the side?"

Roy was very big in the community. He was the pastor of a church, the minister of music at several other churches, a vocal coach, and a minister in the prisons. I'd say between work and me he pretty much had his hands full.

I didn't want to pressure him, but it had been over two years and he had only met Elliot once. That meeting didn't go too well, Elliot didn't take a liking to him. Roy and I were talking marriage, a house and another baby. We were on our Bonnie and Clyde flow! I would do anything for him and he would do anything for me, but little did I know the time for proving that theory was on the horizon.

"You love me?" Roy asked lying in bed heartbeat to heartbeat.

"You know I love you," I voiced, "That's not even a question."

"Would you do anything to make me happy?"

"Where is this going?" I interrupted.

"I just want to know if you're ready to take this to the next level," he continued.

Excited by the sound of that, I sat up and looked him in his eyes.

"Of course, I would do anything to make you happy," I answered, kissing him softly on the lips.

"Ok, I know you can get any man," he continued, "I want you to find someone, let him ejaculate in you, and then come over and let me lick you clean."

Completely thrown off by his request, I asked him to repeat it.

"I want my baby to have it all," he said, "I don't want to hold you back from nothing."

"Ok," I agreed as I laid back down on his chest.

Though I was no stranger to interesting sex experiences, it was odd to me that someone I was talking about marriage with would make such a request.

I spent the next week scoping out my victim, getting him in bed was easy as pie. I did what Roy asked and came over. Damn near tackling me to the floor; he ripped my skirt off exposing the fact that I had no panties on. Submerging his face fully into my pocket he began to lick from the inside out. That night there was something different in the way he made love to me. There was a different level of excitement as he asked all the details that had taken place with Mr. anonymous.

Requests like that became more frequent and extreme; when I would refuse or say I'm tired, Roy had a way of making me feel guilty. He said I was hurting him as all the other women did in his past and that he gave me the world only asking for small favors in return. My heart broke at the fact that I was hurting him, so I continued to comply. Roy took very good care of me. He paid my bills, took me to nice places and kept shopping money in my pocket. He spoiled me like crazy, and because of the message I received early on in childhood; I understood that because I was given nice material things I should automatically know I was loved. I felt the least I could do was fulfil his sexual fantasies, I mean hell I had done it for less.

After a while, things started to get shaky between the two of us. We were on and off in the months that followed and the older I got, the less satisfied with being a secret I became. I mean we were going on being together four years, and nothing had really changed. The sex remained steady in the amazing department, but even that was no longer enough to keep me interested. With me being gone so much and Elliot still being young I had to start letting the cat out of the bag to my close family who kept Elliot while I was spending all this time with Roy. They voiced concerns with the age difference and the secrecy, but there was nothing anybody could say to make me love Roy any less. He was my everything, and I was his, or so I thought.

Chapter Seven

Deception

"Not again!" I screamed kicking the tire of my Honda. This car was always breaking down, and I refused to put any more money into it. Sitting on the curb, the sun blazing on top of my head I decided to call Roy. His shop was only minutes up the street from my school, and I figured he could give me a ride. I called him once, no answer. Called him again and still no answer. Ugh, I guess I'll walk, I thought to myself. Tossing my backpack across my shoulder, I set off down the street. When I reached the end of the road, I saw several news reporters surrounding the building. What in the world is going on, I mumbled? I walked across the street to get a closer look. Maybe this is why Roy wasn't answering my calls.

"Excuse me miss," A reporter called out to me. "How do you know Roy?"

"Uh, I don't," I replied shakily.

Disinterested in sticking around any longer, I hopped on the next bus and headed home. I needed to find Roy and quick.

When I got to the house, I tried Roy on his cell again this time he answered right away.

"Roy, where are you?" Extremely worried I asked. "What's going on?" I continued, "There were news reporters at your shop this afternoon."

"I know," he replied, "I don't have much time, so I need you to listen to me. Do not believe what you hear," he directed, "Just trust me on this one."

"What's going on?" I asked again.

"I'll be in touch," he promised and hung up the phone.

In complete shock, I sat there staring at the ended call when my phone began to ring again. Hopeful that it may be Roy, I quickly answered.

"Sam," a voice called from the other end, "Have you seen the news?

Almost certain it had to do with Roy I hung up the phone, turned off the ringer and tuned into the news.

"Roy Sanford," The news anchor announced. "A local Pastor is accused of raping a 16-year-old girl during her vocal lessons. This is not his first run-in with the law. He was accused twenty years ago of molesting a 14-year-old daughter of a woman he was dating, and again a few years after for raping the teenager who was cleaning his home while his wife was in the hospital."

The news hitting my chest like a ton of bricks, I lost my breath. I couldn't believe what I was hearing, nor did I want to. This had to be a mistake, Roy wouldn't do something like that. I picked up the phone and called him. "You have reached the voice mailbox of..." I hung up. I needed answers, and I needed them now. Not knowing what to believe I quickly pulled up the internet. The news was busting every social media site wide open. There were tons of women coming out about things he had allegedly done to them or women they knew. I spent all night and into the early morning online defending his name against whom I considered lying scumbags.

I called into work the next day and stayed in bed. Hours into the afternoon an unknown number popped up on my caller ID. Waiting to hear from Roy I promptly picked up.

It was Roy, "I'm sorry for all this Sam, I'm not who they are making me out to be," he explained.

"I don't care about any of this," I replied already crying hysterically. "I just want to see you," I begged, "Please, don't shut me out."

"I want to protect you from this," he replied. "They are trying to crucify me. These are just women who wanted to sleep with me, and I turned them down, you must believe me," he pleaded.

I was silent, and puzzled, but I knew that Roy was alone somewhere and no matter what was being said about him, I loved him and wanted nothing more but to hold him.

For weeks, we met up in dark alleys, bug infested motels and spent a lot of time riding around in foreign area's where Roy wouldn't be spotted. We wore skull caps, sweatpants and never parked in one place for too long. He became emotionally needy and needed to make love just about every time we gathered. Old habits die hard I guess. His court dates were lined up, and I planned to be at every one of them, standing side by side letting them females know that he had a solid woman and he didn't need to rape anybody. After his second court date, I was approached by one of his past alleged victims and was given a large manila envelope. Interested to know what was inside, I sat down and opened it. What I found was shocking. Therein lie the court documents from every alleged victim of his past as well as the current young lady's statement. Unable to take my eyes off the paper I read each page line by line. Now sick I ran to the bathroom to throw up. There were many reasons I wanted to stick by Roy, but something in the milk wasn't clean. This current accuser practically cut Roy out and pasted him on the paper. From the way he liked his penis stroked, to his strange fetish with wiping you up with specific paper towels after sex, she described it all. There were things written in the document that a person who had never engaged in sexual activities with this man couldn't possibly know anything about. She explained things that I thought were special between Roy and me, things I thought he only did with me. My heart shattered into a thousand pieces; I could do nothing but cry.

Later on, that night I received a phone call from Roy.

"Did you sleep with her?" I shouted!

"I never raped her," he responded.

"Did you sleep with her?" I asked again, "And don't lie to me!"

He said nothing.

"You must have," I said. "How else would she know our most intimate engaging's?"

Still, he said nothing. I paused and took a deep breath.

"How could he hurt me so deeply?" I continued.

I had been hurt by love in the past, but this was by far the worst. I had given all of who I was, and had been to him.

"How was I not enough?" I could physically feel the aching in my chest cavity.

I wanted to believe what he was saying, I wanted to support him but what would that say about me. Was my self-worth so low that I was willing to look past what he had done to these girls? The questions were coming to my mind faster than I could answer them.

The case got heated, and Roy was facing serious charges due to his history of sexual assault. He was out on bail but put on house arrest awaiting trial. I tried sticking it out because one of my greatest strengths, yet biggest weakness is that I'm loyal to a fault. After weeks of visiting him on house arrest, bringing him food and letting him screw me I started to feel trapped. I wanted out but didn't know how to break free. Maybe this was my way out. Leaving after visiting him yesterday morning, I decided it would be the last time I walked down that road. It was time to finally walk away. He continued with house arrest and eventually went to trial. The verdict was unknown to me because I had moved on to a whole new life. So, this is how it feels to breathe anew?

Poem

Fly high

Spread your wings little birdy you were meant to fly

Spread your wings little birdy go and testify

Of all the things you've seen while traveling your journey

Collecting scars upon your wings, while on this path you were learning

If you're ever asked about the blue skies you so freely roam

Remind them of the dark clouds in which you once called home

Soar high into the sun the sky is yours to conquer

So, spread your wings little birdy you are caged no longer

Chapter Eight

Wolf in Sheep's Clothing

"Come on Elliot," I called out while rushing to the door, "We're going to be late for church."

Church had become a big part of my life after the separation from Roy. I went through a deep depression and experienced suicidal thoughts. Things had gotten so dark for me that I was barely able to care for my baby boy. I started connecting with the Pastor and First lady. Along with help from some elders, I was able to get to a place where I could breathe again. Things were going well for my son and me; we finally had a life of our own with no distraction. I was working, and we had our place, I was heavily involved in the church and working towards figuring out what my purpose was. Though I was not completely healed, and some would say I more or less buried the pain of my newly ended relationship, I was doing well on the surface.

Walking out the doors of the sanctuary that morning I felt good, as I always did when I attended church. Spotting my girls in the corner, I walked over to greet them. I had a little more time to mingle since I was freshly single. We talked and laughed like the good old days, which I really needed, but it came to an abrupt end when Elliot made it known that it was time for him. As I approached the door, I was stopped by Rev. Bryan. He was an interesting guy. Very nice and always respectful but the way he looked at you made your skin crawl. I chopped it down to him just being old. He proceeded to ask me if we could connect to go over some ideas he had for the children at the daycare that he oversaw. Being that I was four years into the daycare world myself, I agreed without hesitation. We exchanged numbers, and I continued out the door. That night he messaged me thanking me for my willingness to help and noted he would reach back out with details.

It had been days, and I hadn't heard anything from Rev. Bryan. Seeing me at church the following weeks he stopped me to inform me that he had been busy and had not forgotten about me. I smiled and went on about my business. Later on, that night I received a call, it was Rev. Bryan.

"I was starting to think you weren't serious about the kids," I joked as I answered the phone.

"I've been extremely busy," he responded.

"How can I help you," I continued?

He went on to tell me how the daycare was suffering, and he was losing families. He wanted to know how to engage the families more, and he wanted some ideas he could try to keep the numbers up. I didn't know much about the daycare or the role he served in connection to it, but I was open to providing suggestions. We brainstormed and came up with a few concrete ideas. As the conversation came to an end, he got silent.

"Hello, you still there?" I inquired.

"Yes," he continued. "I just wanted to ask you something but don't want to offend you.

My heart now racing, I proceeded with caution.

"What is it?" I said.

"How did you end up with a slime ball like Roy?" He said. "Did no one tell you what kind of person he was?"

Now dang near in panic mode, I paused and took a deep breath. It had been some time since I had truly talked about Roy to anyone.

"No one told me because I told no one I was dating him," I replied, "We kept our relationship a secret for four years."

"You know he didn't deserve you right?" He said softly in an attempt to be kind, but it came off sexually awkward.

I was starting to get that feeling I got when I was about to enter a situation that I wasn't comfortable with but didn't know how to halt it.

"Thank you," was all I could produce at that moment.

It was quiet for a moment, and then his voice came through the phone.

"Well thanks again for the suggestions," he added.

Relieved that the call was coming to an end, I verbalized it being no problem and quickly hung up. What was it which made me a candidate for the creeps, I thought to myself?

For the days to follow Rev. Bryan in-boxed me on social media with smiley faces under the pretenses of "just checking on you," he reached out to me like this at least once a day. Uncomfortable with where things were going I reached out to one of my friends from the church who seemed to be cool with him. I met up with her for lunch, and I dived right in. Telling her about the encounters I had with Rev. B and asking if I should be concerned. She looked down at her plate and then back up at me.

"I have gotten the same vibes," she said, "He's even gone so far as to comment on my breast."

Surprised but not completely shocked by what she was saying I started to feel uneasy.

"He's cool," she said, "But he can be inappropriate so be careful."

Leaving lunch that day I began to think of ways I could end communication with Rev. Bryan. I was laying Elliot down when my phone rang. 'Ugh Rev. Bryan again,' I announced, then answered my phone. He was thanking me for the advice I had given him and let me know how successful things were since he implemented some of the ideas. Congratulating his success, I still couldn't shake what Brandi had told me at lunch.

"Let me ask you something," he voiced, "What attracted you to someone so much older than you?"

Not sure why we were back here or why that was any of his business, I said nothing.

"Ok, maybe that wasn't the best way to ask," he declared, "I know you're a great, beautiful woman and I don't feel he did right by you nor did he deserve you."

I sat down on my couch thinking of what to say so that I didn't hurt his feelings, but also so this did not get out of hand. I had a habit of thinking how things would affect others but never myself.

"It's been a long time since I've touched a woman," he persisted, "And I feel there's chemistry between us."

"It's too soon for me," I explained, "I'm not ready to be intimate again. There are still so many feelings I got to work through."

"How about this," he suggested, "We don't have to have sex, we can just do it over the phone."

On the inside I screamed, 'NO!' just before telling him, "Um, I'm not sure."

Why couldn't I just say no and stand on it?

"I understand your resistance," he said, "I wouldn't do anything that would hurt you, I'm ready and I have my hands in my pants," then he whispered, "What kind of panties are you wearing?"

Now sitting at the kitchen table feeding his ego, I could hear moaning coming from the other end. Feeling sick to my stomach I began to talk nasty in efforts to get him off sexually and get him off my phone. Never did I see Rev. Bryan in that manner. In fact, he was very known and liked by all in the church, and because he was good friends with my spiritual father, I had a certain level of respect for him. When he was satisfied, he thanked me in this voice of exhaustion.

"You really are a great woman," he stated right before hanging up the phone.

Not knowing what to make of what just happened, I threw my phone and began to weep. There was no safe place to hide. From the streets to the pulpit, this sex demon followed me. It was me; it had to be. How else could one explain the multiple situations I found myself in? Was I too friendly? Did I have "I'm sleazy pick me" written on my forehead? What was it that made me the target for continuous unwanted sexual encounters? As I'm processing through all my feelings, my phone dinged. There was a message from Rev. Bryan thanking me again and asking for a nude picture so that he could have a visual to hold onto.

There were two more of those encounters before Sunday rolled around, one via phone and second via social media messenger. I stayed home from church that day in the attempt not see him, but that didn't stop him from reaching out. That Sunday afternoon I decided to deactivate my social media accounts and lock myself in my house. Still wrestling my recent breakup and now this was starting to weigh heavy on me and to top it off, my parenting duties did not cease just because I was beginning to feel depressed. The feeling of hopelessness that I had so perfectly mask was starting to resurface.

Knowing I had to get from under the weight I had buried myself in, I sent Bryan a detailed message informing him that I was no longer interested in whatever it was we had going on, but he refused to let it go that easy. He brought back to my memory that he had messages of me engaging in sex talk and pictures that I sent him and if I thought it would end on my account then I had better think again. He reminded me that he and my spiritual dad were friends. He stated if he went to him with the photos and messages I would be in hot water because I already had a reputation for going after older men such as Roy and Mitch. Completely blown away by the fact that he was trying to blackmail me, I shuttered at the fact that he might have been right, why would anyone believe me? He was a well-known Rev, and I was what the streets called a tramp trying to find myself. Hanging up the phone, I knew I would never be able to get out of this on my own; he now owned me.

Dark clouds were cast where light once was. Life had become dark again, and I was certain that God had indeed forsaken me. There's no way I could go through so much and still believe that there was a higher power watching over me who loved me so much. In my following weeks of despair, I didn't seem to know whether I was coming or going but eventually there was a ram in the bush. Cleaning my kitchen, I heard a knock on the door. Upon opening the door, I see my girlfriend Brandi standing 5 feet even, smiling from ear to ear.

"You'll never believe what happened," she announced.

Inviting herself in she wasted no time divulging that Rev. Bryan was just called in for a meeting to discuss his recent exposure of watching porn at the daycare. The daycare was apparently associated with the church in which

Brandi's mom worked in the office and was privy to all the info first hand. She went on to say that they were indecisive on how they were going to handle it. As she rambled on all I could think was... "this is my way out."

"Sam!" She called.

"Sorry, I have a lot on my mind," I said. "I'm not feeling well, thanks for stopping."

Walking her to the door, I couldn't wrap my mind around how I was going to bring myself to tell my dad about what took place between his good friend and me, but I knew that if I didn't do it now, I could potentially lose my opportunity to break away from him.

I set up a meeting the next day, just my dad and me. I told him everything from start to finish including the compromising pictures I had sent. In total shock and heartbreak, my dad expressed his sadness and embraced me. Happy that he could see the truth, I fell into the hug and sobbed. Though Rev. Bryan would soon be a thing of the past, I now questioned everything I believed about the church and its people. It had become clear to me that anybody would betray you given the right situation or circumstance and he proved just that.

Everything I had been sweeping under the rug for years was starting to burst at the seams. I couldn't take another thing on my plate, so I vowed from that day that I would not entertain another person until I was ready to be serious again.

Chapter Nine

Session

The past four years had been a rollercoaster. Finding who I was as a young lady complicated itself when life went from Elliot and me; to Elliot, me and a husband plus two. I had stuck to my vow to wait until I was ready to be serious, but little did I know that moment would come sooner than I expected. 4 months after the ending of Rev. Bryan I met my now husband, William. I know what people may be thinking, it takes more than four months to deal with everything I had going on internally, and boy that is right.

"William, I'm tired of fighting about the same stuff," I argued, "You knew the state that I was in when you married me. I was wounded and trying to find myself. For some reason, you thought you could save me."

We had been married four years. In the beginning, everything was googly eyes, intimate hugs, and mushy kisses, but somewhere down the line things started to get muddy. My past hurts were beginning to show themselves in the way I operated as a wife and mother. I was starting to become callous and resentful. I had this idea of what marriage was going to be like, but because we were two broken pieces trying to create something whole, there was a lot of clashing. The love was there no doubt, and so was the friendship. However, the demons of our past seemed to wage a war that we just weren't winning.

"I feel as though you only give me parts of you," William stated.

Trying to figure out how he couldn't see that's all I had to offer was half of me, I sat back and rolled my eyes in irritation. At this point, it was as if we were now talking at one another and not to one another. Thereinafter, we seemed to throw hurtful words, spend less time together and agreed to disagree on most things. It was almost as if we were just going along to get along.

Sitting in bed one day, it hit me. Maybe William was right. I hadn't dealt with my past hurts, and they were killing my present relationship. For years I battled the bondage that entangled me. I prayed, I meditated, I took medication, I fornicated, I drank, I partied, and I cut.

However, nothing seemed to bind up the gaping holes I had in my heart. So, I stuffed everything into a box deep inside the back of my mind; filling my life with work, church, friends, and family. When I was busy, I felt great, but the loneliness, pain and the nightmares always seem to find me in my alone time. When I met William, he was everything I never knew I needed but I wasn't ready for him at the time, yet we decided to come together anyhow. Engaged thirty days after meeting, pregnant five months after the engagement and married three months after the pregnancy. I guess one could say we wasted no time. It had been hard for me to see the areas in which I had caused our marriage to fall apart. I was so busy pointing out Williams flaws that I forgot to look in the mirror.

Sitting William down that night, I informed him that I was finally ready to go to counseling. There was no other way around the healing process, and if we were going to get the marriage back on track, I had to first shed the dead weight of the skeletons in my closet. Excited to hear the news, William encouraged me and told me how much he supported me. Finding a therapist was easy. I was put in contact with one who was a family friend and had done some work with others I knew in the past. I reached out to set up the first session, and though I was a little resistant, I knew that this was the biggest step in working towards a healthy marriage.

Leaning back on the couch I stared out the window behind her melon-shaped head.

"So, what brings you in?" She asked.

Wondering how many times she asks that a day, I rolled my eyes and stated...

"The same thing that brings everybody else in, I have issues."

Astonished by my response, she sighed and continued to ask me questions that I could have asked myself for free in the comfort of my own living room.

"Why the resistance?" She inquired?"

I bit my lip in annoyance. As much as I knew I needed to be there, I didn't want to be. So, all I could think about was how much my husband better appreciate the fact that I was doing this. The session came to an end, and I was elated.

"See you next week," she announced.

"Yeah, yeah," I returned, dang near running her over to get out the door.

I was so happy to finally make it home. Taking off my shoes I was met at the door with fifty million questions.

"It was the first session, and there's nothing really to tell," I snapped, "I'm tired, I want to go to bed!" walking past William and towards the bedroom.

I continued to go to the sessions in efforts to make William happy, but I wasn't making myself open to receive the benefits of all that therapy had to offer. Until one session we were going over how my recent week had gone. I was telling her about a dance I had coming up and how I was extremely nervous. She began to help me get to the underlying root of my fear and gave me tools to practice to overcome some of the anxiety I was having. We spent the entire session rehearsing the dance and how I was going to handle it. Finally, something not so daunting. I appreciated the time she put into helping me with something that had nothing to do with why I was there.

The more and more sessions I attended, the easier they became. We were starting to connect on a friendship level with every interaction. I had a lot of fears, and she continued to help me conquer them one by one. During this one particular session, I sat across from her excited to see what this meeting had in store, but this time her eyes held a different story. I could read sadness in them, and though I was there to iron out my mess, I took it upon myself to ask her about hers. After all, my dream was to go to school to be a counselor.

"How was your week?" She asked per usual.

"We're not going to talk about me today," I suggested, "Let's talk about you."

"Uh, no that's not how this works," she stated chuckling.

"Why not, therapist needs somebody to talk to also," I insisted.

After much convincing, she began to tell me about her husband and the divorce that they were currently going through. Knowing what it was like to not be in one accord with your spouse I offered empathy. At the end of that meeting, I saw a lighter side of her, not that robot 'do not connect with your client' side I was used to seeing. We all need somebody, and at that moment, I provided the listening ear she needed.

Things started to become personal the more we connected. She would text me to check in on me and to talk me off cliffs when I was having breakdowns. She became a good friend. She encouraged me to go back to school and helped me get in. After doing so, she made sure I had everything I needed to be successful. I was able to call and bend her ear about anything and receive sound advice in returned, and though things were better at home due to my attending counseling, William was not happy with the friendship I had built with Sindy. At the next therapy session, I discussed with Sindy whether she felt the need to refer me out due to us now operating more like friends then professional. She insisted that the friendship we were building would not impede with the level of service she would provide. I must say, having a therapist on speed dial was my saving grace as I navigated through the muck and

mire of my marriage.

The more time I spent with Sindy, the more things became rocky in my home life. I didn't understand William not being happy seeing that he wanted me to go to see a therapist. I was extremely happy with having the escape of a real friend and one who seemed to know me better than I knew myself. For once I felt normal. Sindy was encouraging, uplifting, inspiring and motivated me to do any and everything I desired. She was an overall support system. It was evident that nothing I did made William happy, so I stopped trying. He did his own thing, and I did mine, then we shared in the responsibilities of the children.

Leaving home in a heated discussion, I was happy to be going to therapy. Sindy had a way of getting me to see things in a way that I didn't before. I felt lighter after leaving my sessions. When I arrived at the room where our sessions were held, there was a different ambiance. After getting started Sindy informed me that she had learned a new form of therapy that she wanted to try out. Trusting that she knew what she was doing, I agreed. She explained that it required her taking me back to my childhood and recreating a more positive or pleasant one. Interested in what this would entail, I consented eagerly. She grabbed a children's book out of the drawer and instructed me to lay my head on her lap. Turning on the waterfall, which was my all-time favorite, she began to softly read the book and rub across my forehead. Falling asleep before the book was over, I drifted into a beautiful dream. I dreamt that she was my mother and we were sharing this moment together. Being gently woken up by the calling of my name, I was brought back to the reality that she was not my mother and I was indeed still that same little girl searching for a mother-daughter relationship. When I went home that night, I thought about the story time. I replayed it repeatedly until sleep fell upon me.

The next morning, I was greeted by a grumpy William.

"Things are starting to get fishy between the two of you," William stated.

Instantly irritated, I asked what he was referencing?

"It's not professional for you guys to spend so much time together," he pointed out, "And the sessions are becoming longer and longer."

"Well yes," I responded, "We tend to stay late and talk after sessions, that's not a crime."

Completely dismissing Williams statement, I continued to get dressed for my outing with Sindy. We were going to the falls, and that was my place of peace. Nothing mattered when I was at the falls. Later that evening, William and I continued to fight about my outings with my therapist. I explained to him that she was a great friend and support system and her focus was helping me become a better me so that our family would prosper. William wasn't trying to hear it. I invited him to sit in on a few sessions, so he could see how they went, but he refused.

In the following session, we continued with the new therapy. This time I laid on her lap, and she started with a story about the ocean and taught me calming techniques. Learning calming techniques was essential for me because I had told her in our first sessions that I was not too big on feelings or processing through them. In the past, before I married, I sexed my way through them and so all this discussing and sitting in your feelings stuff was new for me. Midway through the session she stood up and went to sit in the chair across the room. Feeling open and vulnerable I balled up and tried to figure out what I had done wrong. After a few moments, she came and sat back next to me. She then began to ask me questions about my past. For the most part, I was ok with answering them, but when things started to get deep, I would sometimes go to these places that I couldn't bring myself back from. I had some deep dark places I tried to avoid at any cost. She continued with the questions, each one getting more and more detailed requiring the answers to get more and more graphic. I could feel my body starting to tense, my head now shaking back and forth, body swaying to and from in the cradled position. Pulling on my ears, I could feel myself starting to panic.

Anxiety was rising in me, and this was usually the time she would bring me down using grounding techniques, but this time was different, she continued to engage.

My hands stuffed between my legs, I was starting to hyperventilate.

"I need something," I kept chanting.

Lifting her head up from the backward tilted position.

She leaned in and whispered in my ear... "Tell me what you want?

"I need something," I continued, feeling more and more in heat.

"Tell me what you want," she said again.

"Touch me!" I blurted out.

Grabbing me by the face and planting her lips on mine we began kissing intensely and heavy petting. Rubbing in all the places that were meant for my husband she set off a trigger that burned a bridge and provided no way back. Straddling her, she ripped off my shirt baring my breast. I buckled under the passion that flowed between the two of us. Everything was happening so fast, and all I could think about was having a physical release so that I could get rid of all the feelings and emotions I was experiencing. When it was all over, I withdrew to the opposite side of the couch. Trying not to process what had taken place, I continued to pull on my ears. From the corner of my eye I could see her struggling to make sense of what went down, and out of nowhere, she began to bawl.

"Please stop," I asked, not being very good at consoling.

She continued to cry and apologize.

"It's fine," I stated in an attempt to get her to stop with the waterworks.

Finally calming down she expressed her sadness about crossing the line and promised it had never happened before.

Text messages came in from her all night stating how she was going to report herself and close her practice. Not knowing what to say I went to sleep. It had been too much to work through in one night. Rising the next morning, I had the night before playing over again in the back of my mind. I wasn't sure how to move forward so I waited to hear from her so that I could follow her lead. I didn't know what to make of the night before. Further, into the evening I received an appointment invite email requesting a meeting a few days out. I accepted the email and was sure she was going to inform me that it was best she referred me out. Meeting up with her had my nerves in a bunch. She showed up in glasses and a baseball cap, apologizing again. She stated that she still felt she could counsel me and that she had never been in that situation. She asked me how I felt, and I explained that I didn't want to think or talk about it again. I wanted to move on and get back to therapy business and maybe less personal. Agreeing to do so, we had a session that day, and it went well, along with the sessions that followed. Over time things were back to normal, but things at home were at its worse. We had finally decided we were calling it quits as soon as our lease was over. Sindy continued to be a great friend and support. I appreciated everything she did and had much love for her.

One sunny afternoon I linked up with Sindy. She seemed to be a little emotional. She asked me if that night meant anything to me or if that was just me being me. kind of tickled by her statement, I let her know that I was sure. I had grown to love her because she was a good person, but that night had no feelings attached to it. She expressed to me that she had fallen in love with me and that she couldn't stop thinking about me. Not knowing she was in that space all this time, I wasn't sure how to react to that. It was clear that she couldn't disassociate the two. She reached over and rubbed between my legs sending all the wrong feelings to all the right places. I sat frozen. I knew what was about to happen was not in today's forecast. Unbeknownst to me, she had already made up in her mind what she wanted and what she was willing to sacrifice to get it. Going forward we engaged in sexual activity sometimes with my permission. She bought me gifts and took me places under the umbrella of her love for me as friends. Many times, we tried to break things off because we both knew it was not right. However, those sole ties and sex spirits joined us in ways we were never meant to be connected. Once again, I found myself in a situation of sex, lies, and secrets. Not even realizing how things had gotten this far, I was devastated by the fact that I had broken my covenant with God and my husband.

Breaking things off became harder and harder as she would tell me that she couldn't be without me and that she loved me just as much as my husband did. She pleaded with me not to hurt her, making promises of a life together and more love and stability then I had currently. The relationship that we had built was not due to what was taking place in my marriage, but more so what was taking place inside of myself. I was seeking something that I had to realize was never going to be. After dealing with some serious health complications, my husband and I realized that the love we had for each other and our family was worth fighting for, we decided to rebuild what had crumbled over time. This time on a sturdier foundation. In doing so, I knew I had to tell him the truth about Sindy and I before we could continue any further.

Chapter Ten

For Better Or For Worse

I bit my nails in nervousness pulling together my thoughts on how I was going to break the news to my husband. Today was the day I had to sit him down and not only tell him I stepped outside of our marriage, but I did so with my female therapist. The first feeling I felt was terror which quickly moved over to shame which was briefly followed by disbelief.

I laid in bed and listened as my husband moved swiftly around the house putting together something special for our alone time. The atmosphere was still and filled with the aroma of the crisp spring air blowing in from the window. The kids were away at school, and though I knew it should have been a good day of lovemaking, movies, and cuddles, there was something that plagued me. Shut up Sam, just enjoy the day my inner conscious was screaming, but my righteous man continued to cry out, "Be honest, he deserves that." Sitting there battling between what I knew to be right and what I wanted to hide I began to get sick to my stomach. Damn it, just say it already.

"Babe we need to talk," I blurted out.

Did I really just say that? I wondered cupping my hands to my mouth.

He curiously walked into the room.

"Ok, what's up?" William asked in a voice that in any other circumstance would have surely soothed me.

My heart now pounding as I dreaded the fact that I could not take back those five words. I sat there in silence trying to digest the request I had made. Mentally I began to curl up inside myself.

"Is everything ok?" He asked again.

Silence was now ringing louder than any words could at that moment.

"Sam, talk to me!" He demanded, impatience now rising in his voice.

The atmosphere began shifting from serene to dense. I found a spot on the floor and focused in on it. Man, there are so many things I would rather be doing right now, I thought to myself.

"Sam, what is it? Huh?" he again pleaded, "You said we need to talk."

"Uh yeah, there's something I need to tell you."

He sat up, judging by his posture I could tell he was now on edge waiting to hear what was taking me so long to say.

"Is it bad?" He uttered.

"Yes," I replied as I hung my head in my hands.

"Just say it!"

"Give me a second," I demanded.

I took in a deep breath, each second felt like needles filling up in my lungs. After wrestling with it I finally just spit it out.

"You were right about Sindy and me."

The shift in the atmosphere felt like a bomb had been dropped. The impact of his silence was heavy. As he sat up, I tried to explain, but he didn't seem to be interested in what I had to say. There was a mixed look on his face. One of confusion, disgust, and heartache all wrapped in one. You would have thought he saw a ghost. The events that followed were like a rollercoaster ride. There were several emotions expressed in a 5-minute timeframe. At first, there was the initial shock. Then the pacing began and then, how

115

could you? After pacing the room several times, William stormed out the door. I sat on the bed silently wondering if I had made a mistake. He was right, how could I? Some time had passed, and I watched the door waiting for him to burst back through them. Seconds felt like minutes and minutes like hours. Tears began to run down my face as I reached for my phone. I searched his name with hesitation. What exactly am I going to say? I sat up in efforts to pull myself together, hoping to hear his tranquil voice on the other end. "You have reached the voice mailbox of..." I hung up. I instantly began praying, asking God to soften my husband's heart. I hit redial and listened with anticipation as the phone started to ring.

"What Sam?" A stern voice barked from the other side.

"Baby, please come home. Let's talk about it, I can explain," I cried.

"You don't have that right anymore," he said.

"I understand you're upset but please come home," I begged again.

Silence filled the air.

"Hello?" I looked down at the phone only to realize he had hung up.

I called back one last time, and to no surprise there was no answer. I threw my phone and let out a scream.

"God, you promised you'd never leave me nor forsake me!" I continued to cry out, "WHERE ARE YOU, HUH?" I dropped my head and in a small voice proclaimed, "I need you. I need you."

Shortly after the door flung open and I was overwhelmed with relief.

The relief didn't last long as the words, "You have to go," fell out of his mouth.

"I trusted you," he roared, "I held you in the highest regards and treated you like a Queen," with his voice trembling he continued, "I knew it, all the late-night sessions and side trips, there's no way it was simply professional anymore."

Face covered in shame all I could do is agree. He plopped on the couch with his hands in his face.

"I gave you my all. I've never loved another woman the way that I loved you."

I stood up and began walking over to him. Tears poured down my cheeks. Finally making my way to the couch, I reached out to hold him and was greeted with a nudge.

"Don't touch me. You can't just make this go away!" he yelled as he stood up, "Pack your things."

I fell to his feet begging and pleading like a slave to its master.

"No, please William. I don't want to lose you," my words seemed to be falling on deaf ears.

"You've taken me for granted, and now I'm going to show you what it means to lose what you love."

He shooed me off as he walked back towards the door.

"And I'm keeping the kids," he stated as he slammed the door behind himself.

Those last words rang so loud you could hear it atop of the Eiffel tower. They are every mother's worse nightmare. I laid crawled up in a ball, rocking back in forth. You're not taking the children; you're not taking the children, you're not taken the children, I repeatedly whispered to myself. The more and more I said it the more intense the anxiety within me became until I felt something rupture. It was my sanity. I was at the edge of the cliff and had finally jumped. I stood up and slowly walked to the door.

My mind now a Rubik's cube that had been mixed up and placed down was discombobulated but clear about one thing and one thing only. I was going to put an end to this once and for all. The hallway appeared never-ending, and my feet seemed heavy with each step I took, but before I knew it, I had made my way to the staircase. I had zoned out and had only one goal. The long hallway became the staircase, and the staircase became the kitchen. The light from the kitchen blinded me as I walked further into the area. Feeling desolate, I pulled open the kitchen drawer and grabbed the first knife my fingers touched. Before I could lodge the knife into my chest puncturing the very organ keeping my alive, I felt a jolt from the back. The blow was enough to snap me back into reality. I hadn't noticed that I had passed my niece sitting at the kitchen counter on my way to silencing the voices in my head.

"Don't do this, please let it go!" She cried out.

"Let me go!" I screamed at her terrified pleas for me to release the knife. "I don't want to be here anymore."

A second hand now covering mine, a male's voice resounded.

"Let it go, you say you want to work it out," he said, "So let's do it, I'm here."

After catching my breath, I allowed him to lift me off the floor and take me upstairs to bed.

In the middle of the night, I was awakened by the moon peeking through the blinds. Sniffles could be heard coming from the other side of the bed. Sitting up, I just began to cry. Reaching over I grabbed his head, nestled it into my chest and began to pray. We both lifted our head as we closed with Amen. Without thought, he leaned in for a kiss. So many feelings came about, and my heart began to race. I couldn't tell whether we were about to embark on a night of self-soothing sex or just intimacy, but what I did know, I was happy even to have my husband touching me in this way again. That night was filled with so many emotions, but nothing could prepare me for what was to follow in the days to come.

The infidelity plagued our marriage. It slowly started to eat away at our "For better or for worse." Some days our love was enough, and others were filled with "What's love got to do with it?" The light at the end of the tunnel started to fade, and darkness covered what was once radiant. I sat at the kitchen table trying to figure out where it all went wrong, and it hit me. We both had hidden messages that had taken the front seat and was navigating how we were operating. Those messages that I received earlier on in life caused me to sabotage things that were important to me. Though I didn't understand at the time all those deep-rooted issues he had been dealing with, I could now see that we weren't fighting just ourselves. Our relationship problems were much deeper than that, and no matter what we tried, it was impossible to fix because we needed to know "How" to fix our marriage and we had to understand the "Why" of the issues we had separately. This revelation hit me like a dagger in my chest. For the first time, it all made sense. Sitting him down to explain what I was feeling, we both realized at that moment that our greatest work was going to be pulling back the layers of those messages by journeying inward to set the future ablaze.

Doing The Work

Decoding those hidden messages that lurk in the places of our mind that we tend to neglect is the key to stepping into our healing and going forward into new beginnings. We must ask ourselves those hard and uncomfortable questions to really understand how we became who we are. In doing so, you open the door for truth to evict the lies in which were concealed, allowing your heart to be healed and your purpose to be revealed. You must shine light where there is darkness. Here are some of the questions I had to wrestle with during my process:

*What messages did you receive along the way that sat in the driver's seat controlling your life?

*At what point did you give up or tell yourself that you were not worth doing the hard work needed to bring about healing?

*What parts of yourself are you hiding, either out of shame or fear that continues to keep you deceived and in bondage?

*Why is forgiving yourself so hard?

*Why do you feel the need to protect your abuser more than you protect yourself?

*What is self-worth to you and how can you help build your esteem and self-worth after such egregious acts?

*After all you've done and all that has been done to you, do you believe you can start anew? If no, why not?

Feel free to ask yourself the same questions or create some questions that tailor and prompt you to do some deep introspecting. Examining yourself is going to be a big part of your healing process. Uproot the parts of you that are growing like weeds smuggling the beautiful garden that's trying to blossom within you. Remember, when removing lies you must replace them with truth. You are worthy. You are not a victim but a victor. You are not your past. Regardless of what was or even what is, you can always start fresh. What you have to say and how you feel matters and most importantly you are fearfully and wonderfully made.

Breaking myths about Abuse, Assault, and Self Worth:

1) *If you find yourself in a situation that you went into voluntarily initially, you do not have the right to say*

no to unwanted advantages made by peers, authority or significant others. **That's not true**. Your body, your rules. No matter what they say or how they try to make you feel. You have the right to feel and be safe. Your voice matters.

2) *Love hurts:* **False**, Love is a lot of things but pain it is not. If you find yourself being hurt under the umbrella of "love" often, it's time to reevaluate who is providing that "love" to you.

3) *If you don't physically fight back or if your body responds resulting in an orgasm when someone sexually assaults you, then you wanted it:* **This is incorrect.** If you are anything like I was, you can have the tendency to freeze up, say no in a manner that is not stern or you simply say nothing and take it. Finding your voice in scary situations isn't always easy. Also, our bodies naturally respond to stimulation. We are not robots and sometimes orgasmic release happens, but it doesn't make it any less unwanted. Anytime an act of sexual intercourse or sexual behavior in anyway takes place, there should be a clear consent between both parties. (If someone is showing reservation or has flat out said no. Then take the time to heed the stop sign, get an

understanding and proceed in the best interest of both parties).

4) *If you wear something revealing or if you are promiscuous you deserve to be assaulted,* your NO does not matter: **This is so far from true**. NO ONE has the right to do anything to you that you do not give permission. Even if you are mid intercourse and you decide you don't want to continue, YOU HAVE THAT RIGHT.

5) *Verbal abuse and emotional abuse isn't that big of a deal:* **One of the biggest misconception out there because Words hold power.** It is the form of abuse that is most over looked because the victim bares no physical scars, but I am here to tell you that mental scars and damage done to one's heart is one of the hardest things to come back from. We often remember what someone said and how it made us feel long after the situation occurs. This type of abuse leaves long lasting stains that carry on with us even through our adult life. This usually plays on a person's self-esteem and often leads to anxiety, depression and sometimes suicide. If you notice, pimps and abusers usually tend to break their victims down mentally before they ever cross

over to sexual. "You are a whore, no one will believe you", "You're worthless, you should be lucky I'm sleeping with you." Etc.

6) *You're to tainted, there's no way you can come back from your past hurts and choices:* If no one has ever told you or shown you that **this is not true**, hello my name is Shay and I am a survivor/overcomer of physical, emotional and sexual abuse, self-cutting, promiscuity, low self-esteem, no self-worth, prostitution, adultery, and let's not forget I attempted suicide. I stand here today liberated from the dance of life that had me entangled and half way to my grave, now extending an open hand for you to join me. You can, and you will conquer and defeat the lies of your past messages. Let this book be a light to guide you in walking into your healing. Consider me your biggest cheerleader, I believe in you.

7) *You're not worth of anybody's time unless you put out:* **Let's take a moment to flip that around**. Nobody is worth your time if their expectations are that you must put out. Your body should be an accessory not a necessity, and once you do decide to share it. You do not have to bargain for some

one's love, no one should ever be able to buy your love and most importantly just because someone is doing things for you, doesn't necessarily mean it's love. If something takes your happiness, your freedom or your sanity, then you can't afford it. True love starts from within and flows outward. You are the cream of the crop!

Conclusion

For most of us, the hardest part of healing is soul searching. Spending time exploring the innermost parts of our being that may expose those ugly truths is the very thing that will help us understand why we are wired and operate the way we do. Decoding those hidden messages predicated upon a conclusion that was drawn from toxic circumstances is part of the hard work of healing. Although discovering and then sitting in those feelings may make you feel naked, vulnerable and bare, it allows you care for old wounds so that they may heal properly. You see, when you bury the emotional pain, and the pain continues to resurface in different areas of your life, each time it shows up the scab is being removed. When you take the time to deal with your past hurts, confusions, heartbreaks, unforgiveness, etc. you are allowing the wounds to heal correctly. This is a critical piece that we often tend to want to skip over when journeying to the other side. Sometimes that means having to admit that you were abused by your grandfather, molested by an uncle, raped by a pastor or even mentally, emotionally, physically or verbally abused by your mother.

It can make you feel helpless, hopeless and damaged and let's face it, who really wants to feel that way? In a world where we are taught crying is for the weak and only the strong will survive we have built up a wall to keep out the wounded parts that continue to play a role in some of our dysfunctional choices. We get so comfortable in our chaos that we try to block out that child from our past who is broken; running from brokenness will not aid in restoration. You must accept, embrace, love and forgive those broken parts of you so that you may be made whole. Here's the thing, strength comes in when we stand in the broken places and declare we will no longer let them govern who we are today. When you leave dark areas of your life unaddressed, life has a way of dancing in those spaces repeatedly causing you to spin out of control. At the end of every joint you smoke, alcohol bottle, or late-night screw, that you use to cover your pain; your problems will still be there staring you in the face. It's time you decode the clutter that is overshadowing all that you're meant to be. Believe it or not, pain has a purpose, but you must process it which will allow you to propel forward. You are never too far gone to where you cannot be restored. You may have endured somethings that were unimaginable and at times feel unbearable, but I am here to tell you that as long as you have a pulse, you have a purpose. The mere fact that you have breath in your body tells you that you can overcome, but it first starts with acknowledging that you were wounded.

Take time to do the introspective work. Believing that you are victorious, will be the golden ticket that will carry you to the other side known as freedom. There you will find peace, joy, self-love and a fresh start. Ask me how I know? Because I have lived hell and came out on fire. You can't undo what you don't know. Take the time to search out those hidden messages so that you can replace them with truth. Take a moment and take a deep breath. You feel that? That's called purpose! Don't let your past hold your future hostage any longer. The gate to the jail cell is open; you just got to walk through it. To the young lady giving her body away, you don't have to. You are a jewel that should only be worn on the crown of someone worthy. To the woman selling her body because you feel that's all your worth, your worth is not measured between the sheets but rather in what you speak. You are far more precious than jewels, nothing compares to you (Proverbs 3:15). To that precious little girl still carrying around the weight of her father's body and his sweat on her face, I say to you, wash up and stand renewed. Release him for that shall surely free you. You no longer have to be afraid, you have permission to step into your whole self, giving life all that you got, withholding nothing. Lastly, to the person drowning them self in drugs, alcohol, food, and sex; I lift you up. Anesthetizing only prolongs the healing process. It feels good, but feelings are fleeting. Give yourself the gift of true liberation. From this day forward, you are free to rewrite your emotional and mental script. The old messages are washed away and behold all messages can be made new. I don't know where the story will end, but I know it's just the beginning.